in Dr. Etienne's memoir shou.
step by his readers and listeners.
his words, along with those
ave much more to learn from him
d spiritual journey."

uitt,
ducator

ing a church mission trip to Jamacia in
uary 2006, through the sponsorship of
ship, he made his way to North Caro-
and the church have cultivated a deep
colleague, and friend I am inspired by
eloved member of our family.

ique personal expression in which he
h others. Throughout this book, he re-
ulnerable so others may have a clearer
faith journey. Edisson has a compas-
enriches the spiritual pilgrimage of
rdless of the task, distance, or circum-
ging footprints as he walks alongside

te need of kind people with a holistic
others, Edisson Etienne is such a per-
npassion shows a depth of devotion, a
ngth of sacrifice rarely seen. It is his
uides him to reach out to his world."

Haven Baptist Fellowship

Matt Mo:
(soccer (

MW00675707

An Immigrant's Voyage From Haiti to America

Working with Juveniles and Death Row Prisoners

Rev. Edisson Etienne, Ph.D.

Thank you for being a part of my Voyage.

Enjoy your reading!

Etienne (signature)

his
ther
God
he e
dive

full
is fa
ples
eve
nec

hus
tiva
twe
tive
infl
siti
and
and

son
tal
his
ele
circ
Ob
Mo
alw

ISBN 978-1-931117-73-9

9 781931 117739

Rev. Edisson Etienne, Ph.D. - etiennememoir2022@gmail.com

The reflections share
considered a beneficial first
sure those who embrace
continues to counsel, will
he continues his personal a

Ms. Delores Walker Pr
Retired Special Need E

"I first met Edisson du
the summer of 2005. In Jan
Grace Haven Baptist Fellow
lina. Over the years Edisson
relationship. As his pastor,
him. He is in every way a b

Edisson illustrates a u
willingly shares himself wit
veals the willingness to be
understanding of his lifelon
sionate determination that
those of us in his life. Rega
stance, he leaves life-chang
those in need.

The world is in despera
commitment to the needs of
son. The measure of his co
width of generosity and a l
strong faith that gracefully

Rev. Dick Graves,
Senior Pastor at Grace

Chapter One

Life in a Rural Community, Le Curieux

I would like to share with you some key facts about my birthplace, Milot. It is a commune in the northern department or province of Haiti. It is located about twelve miles from Cap-Haitien. It is best known for the Sans-Souci Palace, which is one of Haiti's most revered landmarks. Hence, the Citadelle Laferrière is also considered as one of Haiti's number one tourist attractions.

In the 1800s, Milot was proclaimed the site of the country's first capital by King Henri Christophe. Under King Henri, the beautiful Sans-Souci Palace was constructed from 1810 to 1813. The construction also included the building of eight smaller palaces, fifteen chateaus, several forts and summer homes, as well as twenty plantations, and all owned and managed by the then royal family.

The Palace is the notorious site of King Henri I's suicide in 1820. In 1842, it was destroyed by a strong earthquake and was never rebuilt. Despite its rough shape, it remains one of the most fascinating sites to see in Haiti, resulting in its designation as a United Nations Educational Scientific and Cultural Organization (UNESCO) World Heritage Site in 1982.[1]

As of 2015, Milot's population was 31,992. In the late seventies, however, the population was probably less than half of that. Nowadays, many people are migrating from big cities to smaller ones where the quality of life is much better in terms of less pollution, access to vehicles, and better roads, which facilitate the daily commute.

---

[1] https://bit.ly/3FryZOo - Access date: 5.10.2020

Pregnancy and Disappointment

On January 25, 1976, a wife and mother of twelve children, was six months pregnant, again, with her thirteenth child on her forty-sixth birthday. About three months later, she gave birth to the writer of this memoir, Edisson Etienne, at the nearest medical facility, Sacred Heart Hospital in Milot, which was about five miles from the rural village, Le Curieux.

Below is the house where I spent my first four-to-five years with my family. It was a humble beginning and yet filled with warm love and mutual respect for one another.

Dad: Jacques Napoléon Etienne

Mom: Anne Marie Catherine Dorvil
Etienne

First family Picture in December 1976

From back left: Dad, Jacques, mom, Anne-Marie, 2nd daughter, Dieudonne,
3rd one, Syllotte, the one who transitioned at age 39,
4th one, Leonnise. Second row: 5th child and 2nd boy, Leon,
6th girl, Annessie, she also transitioned at age 53, 7th girl, Daniella.

Front row: 8th child and 3rd boy, Joshua, trying to play with the baby (me),
9th child, a girl, Violette the one touching her chin with left hand, 10th child, a
girl, Lourdy standing on the left side of Violette, the 11th child, a girl, Wilmine,
and the 12th child and last one, Edisson, being held by the 7th girl, Daniella.

3

During our first family picture, the first child, Jean, was the photographer and the second child, Erica, had already passed away at age thirteen from yellow fever.

My dad was fifty-two years old, and my mom was forty-six when I was born. As a result, some people in our community thought I was my oldest brother's secret child as he was twenty-three years old. They could not believe my middle-aged parents were still having children.

From the announcement of my conception to birth, the news of my arrival was surrounded by controversy and disappointment. According to my parents, there was a sadness on everybody's faces. For some members in my family, my birth was a blessing and a curse. My presence was not a welcomed one, as I was considered an extra load.

Mary Elizabeth Ellison

So, what is behind the name of a man who was thrust into this family dynamic? The name Edisson was given to me after a lady named Mary Elizabeth Ellison, who visited with Haitian Baptist Mission from Indianapolis, Indiana. She became my godmother. She was in my rural community visiting some local churches with the Haitian Baptist Mission in the hope to find school children who were excelling academically to support them financially.

First Baptist Church of Indianapolis was very instrumental in the life of my siblings and my education for years. She would travel to the northern part of Haiti every one to two years to visit and keep in touch with everyone's academic progress, while doing other missionary work. Every now and then, her religious leaders would join her in those mission trips to have a first-hand experience on the ground.

My godmother had a master's degree in education and loved reading. As a young boy, I can vividly remember her carrying a book wherever she went and would read while waiting for something. She also liked completing crossword puzzles. She believed that reading and crossword puzzles exercised the muscles in the brain in order to stay mentally sharp.

My first individual picture
I still do not know with whom I was mad!

I have been told that some of my older siblings were furious with my parents for being pregnant, for a thirteenth time, which meant more responsibilities for them. They felt like their youth was being stripped away by caring for their growing number of younger siblings.

My siblings never had the time to be like other teenagers in their community as there were always house chores to be completed. I became an extra burden on their shoulders and in their daily routines. My presence in this world and theirs had created unhappiness and a certain level of resentment, not only toward my parents but also toward me. Once they realized that I was not going anywhere, they had no choice but to accept me as an integral member of the family.

Two decades later, I tried to put myself in their shoes and frankly, I would have felt the same way if I were one of the older ones. For what it is worth, I have never had the experience of caring for a younger sibling.

I became an uncle at age 10. I used to tease my oldest brother by telling him I was an uncle before him, and with no hesitation, he would mock me by saying that being a father was better.

By the time I turned seventeen years old, I had several nephews and nieces. As a teenage uncle, however, I had played the role of a father when one of my sisters and her husband left their first daughter to go to Strasbourg, France, on a two-year scholarship. Upon returning, that niece refused to call my brother-in-law father and said to him, "Edisson is my father. I do not know you." It took her awhile to begin a father-daughter relationship. While examining that experience, it was a nice practice to function as a father figure at an early age.

Sometimes I thought about my parents who had thirteen mouths to feed several meals daily including snacks, which almost certainly required lots of planning and coordination. Looking back, I often wondered if some people in our community thought my parents had a restaurant when they were grocery shopping. Thanks be to God; we never went a day without foods. In fact, we were able to share with others.

2020 Vision vis-à-vis COVID-19 Pandemic

The year 2020 began like any other year with lots of projects to accomplish throughout that year and plans for the next year. One of my plans for 2021 was to have a huge celebration in Deerfield Beach, Florida, for my mom's 90th birthday on January 25, 2021. Our hope was for all of her children, grandchildren, and great-grandchildren to be in attendance for a huge family reunion.

Yet, as we say in the Haitian proverb, "People plan, and God makes decisions." In November 2020, my mom tested positive with the deadly virus, COVID-19, and spent several weeks in south Florida at North Broward Hospital. She recovered without being put on a ventilator. The COVID-19 floor team did an excellent job providing medical care to my mom. They gave us medical updates twice a day. Allowing us to video chat with her every two days, I was able to forward a video to all my siblings and their loved ones.

Overall, my siblings and I were well pleased with the hospital's level of professionalism, communication, compassion, understanding, support, and care for our matriarch. Most of all, they went beyond their regular duties by doing things like allowing us to see her, virtually, through Facetime. It was very comforting to see her because visits were not allowed. She was alert throughout her hospitalization and recovery period. She spent less than two weeks at a rehabilitation center before being discharged to one of her children's homes.

When it comes to our doyenne, all ten of us as her children agreed not to send her to a nursing home. One of Haiti's cultural values is to care for aging parents. We strive to implement this tradition in our country of adoption, the United States of America.

Her medical team was extremely impressed by her determination to live and her mental sharpness. During an interview with local TV station, Channel 7, WSVN on her 90th birthday, Monday, January 25, 2021, her medical doctor said, "She is the oldest patient who survived COVID-19, so far, from that hospital."[2]

Forty-four years later after being pregnant for the last time, that same wife, now a widower after fifty-five plus years of marriage with one husband, mother of ten, grandmother of twenty-eight, and great grandmother of nine, celebrated her ninetieth birthday via zoom at her oldest daughter and son-law's home, Mr. and Mrs.

---

[2] https://bit.ly/32xlGxe - Access date: 2.10.2021

Thomas Konevich in Deerfield Beach, Florida. There were about forty electronics connected, and over 150 people participated.

My mom, her oldest daughter, Dieudonne, and her husband, Thomas Konevich

My mom's 90th birthday picture

The Art of Raising Thirteen Children

My mom was sixteen years old, and my father was twenty-three when he asked her parents' permission to date her, and he was turned down. Then, he sent his father to go and ask on his behalf.

They dated for five years and then made their vows to love each other until death separated them. After their humble honeymoon, they began talking about children. My mother wanted one, and my father three. During their debate, she told him being pregnant and giving birth seemed too painful and she would prefer to have only one.

Apparently, none of them kept their end of the honeymoon bargain because they spent over two decades having children: nine girls and four boys, of which I am the youngest. They buried their second child, Erica, at the age of thirteen after she suffered with yellow fever.

They became popular in their local church where they were known as "baby machine parents," as my mom was pregnant almost every two years. Their late pastor jokingly threatened to stop officiating the baby dedication ritual after their seventh one.

Whether they were influenced by their pastor or not, both agreed to visit a family physician to discuss some birth control methods. As a result, her tubes were tied. Months later, it appeared the procedure was successful.

To make a long story short, they became pregnant again. "Honey, we are not going to see anymore medical doctors. I believe God is trying to send us a message that we will stop having kids in His appointed time," my father said. That appointed time came after having five more children for a grand total of thirteen.

My dad used to say that God has a sense of humor by putting number one in front of three to make thirteen. My mom, on the other hand often says that she could have ended up with eighteen children due to some miscarriages. One may conclude that my parents were extremely busy.

However, when it was time for me to be taken to church and go through the ritual of baby dedication, one of my late older sisters, Syllotte, carried me instead of my mom to avoid religious embarrassment and church gossiping. Some fellow parishioners can be cruel, without realizing it, when it comes to gossiping about other people's personal business.

My parents began having girls for a while after their oldest son and it did not take long before they started debating whether or not girls' ears should be pierced. My dad was against that idea, but my mom thought otherwise.

"If God wanted girls' ears to have holes He would have sent them like that," my dad argued. My mom, however, waited until my dad was deployed as a soldier, and pierced those girls' ears. My dad, upon his return, was not pleased with the decision but it was already done.

My parents took their wedding vows with reverence and seriousness. They went through some challenging times in their emotional voyage but never let challenges interfere with their love for each other and their mutual commitment to work things out between themselves. They worked as a team to raise respectful and responsible citizens. They used to tell us, "Our goal is to raise world class citizens."

My father was a true and consistent gentleman. Throughout my observation of him living with my mom, he always put his wife and family needs first before his. He was a loving caring husband, father, and a good active listener. He was always present and ready to assist when needed.

Wedding Vows Renewals and Life's Celebration

For the renewal of their fiftieth wedding anniversary, we, the children, bought new rings for them to exchange during a religious ceremony at their local church, Église Évangélique d'Haiti de la Rue 12 E, Cap-Haitien, Haiti, on Saturday, December 20, 2002. My father was an ordained deacon and a ministerial advisor to the senior pastor, Reverend Mégie Sylvain.

The late clergy, Reverend Dantus Louis, who officiated my parents' first wedding was also present and participated at their vow renewal ceremony, which he considered as a ministerial hallmark. My older sister and I were the ring bearers. We thought about hiding those rings like it happened with toddlers sometimes just for fun. After the celebration and reception, we sent them on a honeymoon weekend.

Some of us went to the hotel with them just to check them in and make sure everything was in place as requested. As I was assisting my dad to undress, due to his Parkinson's disease, I jokingly asked him if he wanted me to use the extra bed in the room to keep them company (if and when they needed something). "I do not know, son. I think you should ask your mom," he answered.

My parents' 50th Wedding Anniversary

Upon asking my mom, within seconds, she said, "Yes, you can stay if it is your honeymoon." We all laughed and kissed each other, and my siblings and I left.

After returning from their honeymoon, they were interviewed by two local Radio stations, Evangelical Voice of Haiti (4VEH) and Cap-Haitien Radio (also known as Radio 4VKB), about their emotional journey and their secret for a successful marriage.

Their fifty-fifth wedding ceremony was held on Sunday, August 3, 2008, in Deerfield Beach, Florida, at Jehovah Shammah Missionary Baptist Church where my oldest brother, Jean, is the senior pastor.

As the youngest child, one of my assignments was to help my dad with dressing up due to his physical limitation triggered by Parkinson's disease so that he could be ready on time for his and my mom's fifty-fifth wedding anniversary ceremony.

The Last Dollar Bill

Upon completing my task, he made a right-handed gesture signaling me to come closer to him and whispered, "I need money to put in my pocket." I reminded him that there was no need for money because it was an anniversary celebration and not a church service. "Son, I do not want to leave without having money in my pocket," he argued. My dad's philosophy was that people should not leave their house moneyless to go anywhere because you never know what might happen and need to buy something.

Anyway, I looked at him with a smile and pulled out my wallet and realized I only had one dollar. I told him that I would quickly go to the nearest Automated Teller Machine (ATM) to withdraw money because I only had one dollar since I mostly used my debit card. He told me that there was no need to go to an ATM and I could just give him that one dollar and he thanked me.

Once my mission was completed, so I thought, he stood up and felt his back pants pockets and suddenly had a puzzled look on his face and asked me for a handkerchief. He used to carry one in his pocket religiously because his underlying principle was that he might need it to clean his reading glasses or just simply give it to someone who might need it.

It was not planned for the oldest and the youngest child to be clergies. He and I officiated the wedding anniversary renewal ceremony. Being one of the officiants of my parents' fifty-fifth wedding anniversary was one of the greatest hallmarks in my ministry, particularly, saying to my father, "Now you may kiss your bride."

My parents' oldest adult grandchildren, Woodley and Emily Etienne were the ring bearers. Families, relatives, and friends joined the celebration. It was a family reunion where people were able to connect and reconnect. The Florida governor, Charlie Crist, at that time sent a congratulatory letter to my parents for that extraordinary emotional milestone.

My parents' 55th Wedding Anniversary

Weeks later, I found that same dollar I gave him in one of that suit's pockets he wore for his formal vow wedding renewal ceremony. I noticed that dollar bill had the number seven on all four corners. That was my dad's favorite number. Subsequently, I decided to keep this dollar bill as a keepsake as it was the last money I gave him before he went to be with God about ninety days later on Friday, November 28, 2008, at age 84. Even during his last days on this earth, his mind was pretty sharp. He was fully aware of everything and was able to make his medical decisions.

With the Holy Spirit's help, I delivered the homily at his home-going ceremony. The title was, "How Long Will Our Dash Be?" It was based on Psalm 90 verse 10, "Our days may come to seventy years, or eighty, if our strength endures; yet the best of them are but trouble and sorrow, for they quickly pass, and we fly away."[3]

My dad's senior pastor, Reverend Mégie Sylvain, and mentee shared concern about my emotional ability to preach at my father's funeral service and volunteered to do it himself. I told him that nobody knew my father better than me and I was ready for that challenge. We, then, both agreed to split the thirty-minute slot into two parts.

It was one of the most difficult things I have ever done in my life and yet the most memorable one. I shared how the line between my dad's year of birth and death was small and yet long and significant based on a life well lived and by the presence of all those who attended.

The homegoing service was held in a mega church, Église Évangélique d'Haiti, Rue 12 E, in our hometown, Cap-Haitien and it was packed. Because my father was formerly in the military, a

---

[3] https://bit.ly/3FvqbY8 - New International Version (NIV)
Access date: 3.1.2021

representative of the police force came to pay their respect to a man who served his country.

He was later laid to rest in the family historic house back-yard in Le Curieux on Saturday, December 6, 2008.

My dad was a giant with a gentle heart, strong but humble, and constantly was prepared to share his personal faith in God through Jesus Christ. He was well respected wherever he went. He treated people with respect and dignity regardless of social and religious class. Always eager to give a helping hand, he prayed with those in crisis as a way to provide spiritual comfort.

Let the Genealogy Begin!

Before I begin sharing my journey as an immigrant working with the North Carolina Juvenile Justice System and a Death Row Prison, allow me to introduce my pedigree so that you may have a better understanding.

My grandparents from my mom's side did not want their daughter to date a soldier because of their oldest daughter's experience. She married a soldier who was living a double life by having a secret child before marriage. Sadly, his deceit continued with other women.

My grandparents from my father's side were exceedingly popular as my grandfather was the well-known butcher not only in his community but also in the surrounding towns. If having popularity was a test of someone's character, my grandfather would have failed because through his fame, he ended up having children all over the place. It has been reported that he was the kind of person who would try to be in a relationship with a mother and a daughter at the same time if able.

My grandmother from my mother's side sold alcohol to make a living but forbade her children to drink it. One day, one of her children confronted her hypocrisy for not allowing her to drink it. She told them that drinking alcohol could slowly destroy one's life and that was her reason for discouraging them from drinking.

My parents grew up with little to no education, but they were determined for their children to surpass them in every aspect. They considered formal education as number one in their parenting bucket list for their children. They also realized that education was the best way to make an honest living and have a better life while having a peace of mind.

My oldest brother made local history when he became the first person in our rural community, Milot, to graduate from high school and go to college. My parents were thrilled and felt like they were the ones receiving that diploma.

Within the Haitian culture, for instance, when a child is successful, most parents feel like it is theirs, too, and the contrary is true. After living in different countries and reading about global family cultural differences, I am inclined to conclude that it might be universal when it comes to parents' excitement vis-à-vis their children's academic achievement.

Educating women during her generation was not a priority. As a result, my mother, Anne Marie Catherine Dorvil Etienne, was a full-time homemaker, local produce seller, and clothes designer for her children as well as those in our community.

We talked with her about the importance of learning to print her name, and she agreed for us to teach her. I will never forget the excitement in her eyes when she finally was able to spell and print her name on her own. It was a lightbulb moment.

On the other hand, my dad, Jacques Napoleon Etienne, after completing his elementary education, dreamed of climbing the higher education ladder. His father, Leon, who was a well-known businessman in our community and neighboring towns told him to join the Haitian army instead, which he did.

My dad, however, believed in continuing education, whether formal or informal. He loved reading. One day during a father-and-son fellowship, he told me, "Son, the moment you stop reading is when mental growth ends. Reading helps people to know places and things they never knew existed. It also sharpens one's mental thinking, reasoning, and allows them to view things in context."

He continued, "In order for you to stay grounded and up-to-date with the world, there are three things you should do daily: read your Bible to keep you in line with God and people, read the newspaper to stay informed with current local, national, and international social affairs and keep the most recent dictionaries nearby if there are new words that you do not understand." Remember, he added, "You need to change your secular dictionary yearly to become familiar with innovative words; however, the Bible does not change but you will also need a very good Bible dictionary."

He spent about fifteen years in the Haitian army and became a very disciplined gentleman in every aspect of his life. He was determined, with God's help, to be and remain faithful to his wife and his family during his military deployment in different towns and provinces in Haiti.

My mom was the disciplinarian in the household whether dad was present or not. Nevertheless, she was in charge most of the time because of my father's career. As a result, she had to wear two hats to make sure order and discipline existed especially during my dad's absence.

She would spank just to send a message to some of the rebellious children. When it came to spanking, however, my dad would use his facial expressions as a way to discipline or just as a reminder that one needed to behave in an acceptable or proper way. With just one look, we knew what we did wrong and how to make things right.

While deployed in Haiti's capital, Port-au-Prince, he would go to a small local restaurant to eat lunch. One day, the owner, loudly said, "I am looking for a military man to help me in expanding my business and I will take care of that man emotionally."

My dad said that he paused and looked around and realized he was the only person in military uniform eating, pondered for a few minutes, and concluded that lady definitely was talking to him. As a result, he stopped going to that restaurant to avoid any further contact because he left his wife and children back home and did not want to jeopardize his family relationship with anybody.

Bear in mind, his dad was not a good role model for him. My grandfather was well known in the community as the butcher, traveling meat seller, and a womanizer. He had children in different neighboring communities but did not have any with his wife.

My dad was not pleased with his father's emotional lifestyle and the way he used women and showed no respect. He thought there must be an alternate lifestyle than the one his father had exposed him to. He was determined to be faithful in marriage. Consequently, he kneeled down and asked God for help and guidance so that he did not become like his father. His prayer was answered because he was the only man among his brothers who was married for fifty-five plus years and had thirteen children with one lady until death separated them on Friday, November 28, 2008.

My dad was a devout Christian, a family-oriented person, and an active ordained deacon. One day, his bishop urged him to attend a local Bible school to become a clergy and he told him that he did not feel God's calling to go to a seminary. He practiced his faith everywhere he went. He introduced us to God and serving others at an early age. My family was incredibly involved in our local church.

He would create or use any opportunity to share his practical faith in God through Jesus Christ with people. He never met a stranger when it came to reaching out to others on his earthly journey. He believed all followers of Christ should share God's love for humanity though practical living.

One day, while on duty at a local military base, my dad saw a group of Christians and they told him that they were going to his house to pray with his family, as it was the custom. He told the group leader that his wife would probably be busy with the children and house chores. He suggested they pray with him. He did not close his eyes as he was on duty. Everything went fine; or so my dad thought.

Days later, he was called in to the commander's office. The commander rebuked my dad for allowing those "Christian people" to pray in front of a military base. Subsequently, he told my dad that he would be court martialed and spend six months in jail.

My dad was a critical thinker and skilled when it came to assessing a situation in a brief time to draw a conclusion. He paused for a moment and told his supervisor, "Sir, Father Thomas from the local Roman Catholic Church could have talked to me directly instead of coming to you, and frankly that was a cowardly act."

"How did you know it was he?" The commander inquired. "During the prayer time, I did not close my eyes, and I saw him pass by and stop to observe what was going on," my dad answered.

He continued by saying, "Sir, if you do not mind, I would like to offer another option, I would rather resign instead of spending six months in jail for the gospel of Jesus Christ. Also, I would like you to know that my God will provide." His resignation letter was accepted, and he was discharged from the army.

After listening to my dad recount that story as a teenager with a twentieth century mindset, I told him that allowing some people to hold a worship service while on duty was not appropriate. We laughed about the whole situation, and he said that he felt that was the proper decision at that time.

Finding New Career, Family Traditions, and Dream Big

Months later after my dad left the army, a local natural juice company, Conserverie Nationale Société Anonyme (CONASA) in Cap-Haitien, was looking for a full-time security agent and he was hired. With my parents saving money they bought a house in Cap-Haitien and allowed a relative to live in it at a minimum cost.

My parents worked extremely hard to provide for us. Even though we lived a humble life growing up, they were known in our community as people who were always ready to share their crops with neighbors, which they considered a way to minister to them.

Living on a tropical island meant there were fresh fruits and vegetables throughout the year. Everything grew organically. During summertime, my dad would take us to his farm to pick-up mangoes from our own tree. Each child had his or her own mango tree, which was unique and interesting because we had opportunities to eat different flavored ones and shared with each other.

My dad was in charge of his family's religious and spiritual wellbeing, and he was consistent and creative at it. He remembered all family members' dates of birth and never missed one. For instance, when my birthday was coming up in early April, he would say something like one week prior, "It is a good thing I do not have anybody who was born in April." That was his way of telling his children he knew your birthday was near and he remembered. With their limited resources, my parents would make each child's birthday feel like the most important one.

A typical birthday celebration was a time to reflect and meditate on God's blessings and especially on the gift of being alive and healthy, as there were other children who passed away young or who did not have parents to celebrate with them.

Then, we would read an age-appropriate Psalm from the Christian Holy Scripture, have a short devotional meditation, eat whatever was prepared, sing the "happy birthday" song, and fellowship with one another. My older siblings note that I was always ready to volunteer to lead the reflection part during the birthday celebration undeterred by my stuttering.

Mom, on the other hand, only remembered her oldest son's birthday. Her consistent explanation has been and still is, "I will always remember the person who introduced me to experience, the excruciating pain, of giving birth naturally."

All my siblings attended elementary school in our community and neighboring ones for high school. My older siblings told me when it was time for me to go to pre-school, I told my parents that I did not want to go to a rural school. I preferred to start my schooling in a big city, Cap-Haitien.

Fortunately, my parents had already bought a house in Cap-Haitien, and my dream to start my academic journey in a big city came to reality. We officially migrated there in the summer of 1980, and I was sent to the nearest preschool, Cœur Immaculée de Jesus, led by Madam Estravius Nicolas better known as Madam Vivi's school in town.

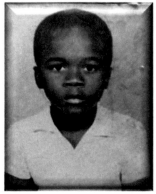

Months before my scholastic voyage began

First day of kindergarten

21

Chapter Two
Migrating to a Big City, Cap-Haitien
with Big Dreams

My dad commuted, daily, by bicycle for work from Lecurieux to Cap-Haitien, which was about 12 miles. My dream to start my schooling was considered as a sign to migrate earlier than expected to reduce his travel distance tremendously.

First of all, allow me to introduce you to my new town, Cap-Haitien. It is a town of about 190,000 people on the north coast of Haiti and capital of the northern province. It is the second largest province after Port-au-Prince, Haiti's capital. It was previously named Cap-Français, initially Cap-François, and Cap-Henri during the rule of king Henri I. It was historically nicknamed the Paris of the Antilles, because of its wealth and sophistication, expressed through its architecture and artistic life.

It is worth noting that Cap-Haitien's population may have doubled after the January 2010 catastrophic magnitude 7.0 earthquake, in which the epicenter was in Port-au-Prince, the capital. As a result, thousands migrated to the northern part where was no devastation. Before the earthquake, Port-au-Prince was the educational center for higher education and afterward Cap-Haitien became the place many parents felt comfortable sending their children after successfully passing the high school government exam.

It is known as the nation's largest center of historic monuments and a tourist destination. The bay, beaches and monuments have made it a resort and vacation destination for Haiti's upper classes. When it comes to tourism, it has also attracted more international tourists as it has been isolated from the political instability in the south of the island. Its most popular beach destination, Labadee, serves as a brief weekend getaway.

To me, the most monumental place in Cap-Haitien is Vertières. It is at that location that the last and defining revolutionary battle took place on November 18, 1803, which was led by the Haitian army general Jean-Jacques Dessalines, and they defeated a French colonial army led by the Comte de Rochambeau.

Bear in mind, the French army was the most powerful one in the world. As French soldiers were being killed in a rapid pace, the French had no choice but to pull out their remaining 7,000 troops from the island and the Dessalines' revolutionary government declared the independence of Haiti on January 1, 1804. Consequently, Haiti became the first brown country in the world to be free from slavery.

Parenting, Protecting, and Pro-Active Providing

Enough history about my hometown for now. While living in Cap-Haitien, my dad worked for a local company CONASA that exported organic fruit juice worldwide. As a boy visiting my dad at work, I vividly remembered seeing big trailers lined up to transport those sealed boxes to different ports of entry in Haiti to be exported.

My father worked with CONASA for about thirty years until he could no longer work and received no retirement benefits. The private retirement system in Haiti is nonexistent and as a result, there is no such thing as a "retirement age." Most people work until they can no longer physically do so, which is a sad reality.

A situation like that makes it almost impossible for college or university graduates to join the workforce unless they have a connection in the private sector or government system to be hired. As a result, many parents work hard, spending all their resources on their children's formal education. That approach can be seen as a form of retirement investment with the hope their children would take care of them when they could no longer work.

My parents also owned several pieces of land, hired people to work on them and shared the crops. During harvest time, I can vividly remember my dad using public transportation from Lecurieux to a bus station in Cap-Haitien, which was approximately a thirty-minute drive.

Then, he used the back seat of his bicycle to transport those goods to our new home twice a month. Also, once a week, with his direct supervisor's permission, he used the back seat of his bicycle to carry a fifteen-gallon plastic drum, weighing 230 pounds, to bring purified water home for us to drink because the government water supply system was not potable.

It seems that providing drinkable water in a country can be a challenge. Case in point, Flint, Michigan, United States, was in a public health crisis from 2014-2019 due to the lack of useable water. According to Wikipedia.com, "Flint's water system was contaminated with lead and possibly Legionella bacteria and between 6,000-12,000 children were exposed to lead. Some scientist concluded that children are particularly at risk from the long-term effects of lead poisoning, which can include a reduction in intellectual functioning and Intelligence Quotient(IQ), and an increased chance of Alzheimer's disease."[4]

After living in three countries and based on my universal observation, I am inclined to conclude that governments can only provide useable water, but it is up to citizens if they are able to provide purified water in their homes.

During the Flint, Michigan water crisis, I came to appreciate more my dad's sacrifice in providing purified water for his family. Being influenced by my father's action, I buy purified water everywhere I go. About thirty-five years later, I make sure my home has a distilled water cooler for my family to use.

---

[4] Wikipedia.com - Access date: 12.20.2020

Anyway, when it came to house chores, I never saw my dad in the family kitchen cooking or even washing dishes or taking our trash. However, he was a very caring, loving, proactive provider, protector, patient, a sharp thinker, and good active listener. When he came to providing for his family, he was a proactive provider travelling to the countryside to pick-up groceries as our food pantry was running low.

After reading about world history from many cultures, house chores were the affairs of ladies back then and gentlemen were the sole breadwinners. It seems to me that the pendulum is shifting tremendously in terms of house roles nowadays. Many men are staying home, caring for their children more than ever before, whereas women work.

Many traditional people, however, do not like the way the pendulum is shifting. They still think that household chores belong to women and men should be the financial provider. Unfortunately, those people will be left behind with their level of thinking because the pendulum will keep shifting further and further from the traditional household system.

At the end of his working day, my dad would sit on his rocking chair and would invite the younger ones to take turns sitting on his lap and sometimes all of us at once. Every now and then our mom would remind him not to have so many on his lap and he would respond, "I will be fine; they are not too heavy."

Growing up, my dad had a few duties around the home. One of them had to do with making sure our teeth were brushed twice daily and especially before going to bed. He thought evening was the most crucial time for brushing after we spent a full day eating several meals and snacks. If he returned home after we were asleep, he would ask our mom if we had brushed our teeth before bed. If the answer was no, maybe, or I do not remember, he would go to our bedroom, open our mouths, and smell our breath to determine if we had brushed our teeth or not before retiring to bed.

Additionally, he would wake us up in the middle of the night to help us pee to avoid wetting on our bed. Sometimes, we would lie to him by telling him we did not need to pee because we did not want to interrupt our sleep. "Ok, let me call the pee for you, Shoo …shoo… shoo." He would make that sound with his mouth several times. Lo and behold! In no time, we started peeing.

I did not know that making the sound, "shoo," with one's mouth could trigger someone to pee and had a scientific explanation for it. During my chaplaincy residency at WakeMed Health and Hospitals, Raleigh, North Carolina, I witnessed a nurse turn on a water faucet slowly for a few seconds and make the noise "shoo" in a patient's room after he reported that he could not pee, and voilà, that patient was able to pee.

My dad would find blessings in any little thing to express his gratitude toward God, his wife, and his children. For instance, after belching or passing gas, he would give God thanks because some people, for some medical reason, could not do so. Also, he would thank his wife or anybody who played a role in preparing a meal for the family.

While reflecting on my father's role, I have concluded that he was a father with a mission to make sure his family was safe and protected. He was a great parent, provider, and protector. He always wanted to know that his wife and children were well taken care of first and foremost.

The School System and Its Methodology

I attended a preschool, an all-boys' school for my elementary education, Marius M. Levy, and a co-ed private Baptist school, College Pratique du Nord, for secondary education. I was involved in extracurricular activities in the latter school. I served on class committees, played trumpet in the marching band, and assisted with chapel services.

During my first trimester as a third grader, I was sick for several weeks with a fever and chicken pox, which kept me home from school. Unfortunately, internet was non-existent, which meant there was no remote learning available. School assignments had to be picked up from the school in order for me to complete them with the help of some of my older siblings.

I was miserable and bored at home after the first week and I missed my friends from school. I prayed and asked God to help me to not ever become sick again because I was tired of staying in my room with no one to play with.

Sadly enough, I had failed third grade, which meant I had to repeat that grade. I received a good spanking from my mom. My dad, on the other hand, used a completely different approach by having a long talk with me. "Son, did you know that you just wasted your mom's and my money for a full year?" I innocently asked what he meant. "Failing a grade is a waste of money. Your mom and I will have to find money to pay for that grade twice. I hope that never happens again because you are a smart boy," he explained.

The Haitian school system was and unfortunately still is about theory with no practice. Students learned about many things that we had never seen or touched. I believe the education system needs to be amended to meet the international educational standard.

There was a time in my elementary education when I hated school. I felt like there was a mental overload of information to study and remember for exams with no practical experience. It is a one-size fits all educational system. Many students, unfortunately, have to adapt in order to survive the structure, pass all subjects, and go to the next grade.

After making my frustration known in my family, one of my older sisters, Leonnise, who worked as a professional photographer, decided to pay a private tutor to assist me with some of the subjects I was struggling with. I must mention that sister, who was like a mother to me, was a high school dropout. She did not want her little brother to make that same mistake she made years ago. I will always consider her as someone who probably saved my academic future.

The Stuttering Boy

As a boy, it did not take long for my family to realize that I had a speech impediment, stuttering. I had extreme difficulty expressing myself without stuttering between words. Simple mundane communication became challenging and bothersome.

I can vividly remember how some of my classmates teased me relentlessly. Some children can be heartless toward peers with any form of disabilities. My family, however, was very understanding and comforting in helping me overcome that challenge.

When it came to schooling, my biggest challenge was reciting some of my lessons in front of my teachers. I would repeat a word multiple times and by the time I moved to the next sentence the cycle repeated all over. As a result, it seemed as though I did not prepare for my oral exam.

Culturally speaking, I am yet to meet a Haitian who would not try to share some natural medicines if you were to tell him or her that you had an ailment. Most Haitians usually have medicines for almost everything.

As it is common in Haiti, relatives and family friends, started sharing all kinds of tips or medicines with my parents for the stuttering to stop. For instance, scream or shout at me every time I began stuttering, drink water from a cow or goat horn, eat cassava powder, or put clean small gravel under my tongue while at home when talking. None of those "remedies" worked. Frankly, it felt like they made things worse.

The truth was all those people who had given my parents those remedies meant well but with no result. I am still puzzled by them and wonder about the origin of those medications and suggestions.

With no solution to my predicament, I learned to live with my stutter and continued life as normal, pretending I was like everyone else. Pretending does not mean the problem has disappeared. I first felt the negative impact of my speech impediment as a teenager when I was interviewed for a radio presenter position at a local Christian Radio station, 4VEH, Evangelical Voice of Haiti. Though I had the formal training in communication, I was turned down because of the stuttering issue.

I was determined to overcome that problem. There is a solution for almost everything as long as one keeps searching. I thought it was possible to find a realistic remedy without all the extra, afore-mentioned rubbish.

At first, I thought I was the only one going through this predic-ament. With research, I discovered it was a worldwide problem. In that research, I learned that stuttering is a communication disorder. I learned to speak a little bit slower than usual while mentally draft-ing my speech. The key is to avoid being excited when speaking. Reducing the speed worked for me, and still does.

Looking back, it was not easy. I wanted to speak at the same speed as everyone else. Almost three decades later, I have to re-mind myself, each time I feel like being excited during a speech I am delivering, to slow down.

House Chores, Breakfast Man, Juice Man, and Supper Man

As the youngest in the family, I have had the privilege to travel with dad on the back of his big bicycle on a regular basis; for instance, going to church on Sundays sometimes in our hometown, Cap-Haitien, or our former churches in Le Curieux or Milot.

Those days were fun. My dad would take his time to show me places and buildings as we journeyed along. I still can hear him saying, "Son, hold on tight to my waistline and let me know whenever you need a break to stretch your legs or pee and I will stop." Reflecting on those days made me realize that he wanted to make sure I enjoyed every moment, which I did.

My dad was always on time everywhere he went, especially, to church for fellowship and communal worship. He considered going to church as the most important meeting and one should be on time out of respect for fellow congregants.

As the youngest in the family, I had several house chore responsibilities. One was to clean everybody's shoes during the weekend and polish them for the following week. It was fun because I could observe the transformation from dirty shoes to shiny ones. There was a feeling of accomplishment and satisfaction after finishing those tasks.

Drinking natural juice was part of our family daily diet. By the time I became a teenager, I was considered the juice master and it became another chore. Everybody liked my juice when I made it. All those compliments boosted my confidence and self-esteem. I felt like I was making a positive impact in my immediate community. At the end of dinner, that juice jar became empty.

My mom sold products at a public local marketplace during the day and came back home in the evening. Somehow, she knew whenever the juice was prepared by me even though she was not present. Mom, what is unique about my juice? I asked her one day. "Your juice taste is always consistent. I can taste the fruit flavor, and the amount of sugar used is perfect. Your juice is never too sweet or needs more sugar. I like drinking your juice at the end of a long working day. Keep it up, my son!" she responded with some kudos at the end.

Fast forward to about twenty-five years, three of my chores in my family has to do with breakfast, making juice, and preparing super. Interestingly, my three boys know if I have made juice after their first sip. We are intentional when it comes to eating meals together as a family. Cooking breakfast, making juice from scratch, and preparing supper are some of my chores in our home, my boys call me " breakfast man, Juice man, and supper man."

Convenience Store and Life's Lessons

After going to the public market daily for a while, my mom decided to open a convenience store in the side of our house where she sold groceries. She was known in our neighborhood as someone who would not turn down a person regardless of his or her ability to pay especially if those neighbors had children to feed.

One day, as her bookkeeper, I was going through the list of her debtors. I asked why she kept selling to those same people who had not fulfilled their debts. "Son, those children needed to have something to eat after school; therefore, it would be heartless to say no to those parents," she wisely explained.

My mom was exceptionally good at math and sometimes would point out some of my mistakes. For instance, she would ask me to complete a math calculation but knew exactly what the result was supposed to be. I was impressed by her level of reasoning and smartness.

She was known by her wholesalers as a woman who was always on time in honoring her debts when I went to pick goods on weekends to take back to her store as that was part of my job description as a bookkeeper. My inventory tracking method had to be on time in order to keep business flowing.

One evening, after completing my schoolwork, I went to the store to help out to give my mom a break after a long day. A young girl bought something. After giving her the item, I extended my right hand to collect the money, and suddenly she scratched the middle of my palm and smiled. As I started to rebuke her for doing so, she ran. I explained to my mom what happened after she overheard the commotion.

Then, she informed me that girl just told me that she liked me. "Mom, what did the scratching of my palm have to do with love." I innocently asked. "Son, culturally, that what it meant when a girl or boy did that to each other." She took time to educate me.

My mom was the embodiment of pragmatic ministry in our neighborhood vis-à-vis those who were in dire situation either to feed their children or themselves when it came to groceries. One day, for instance, right after dinner was cooked she told me to deliver a meal to a mother who had a daughter (who was physically challenged) in our community. I told her that I would do so after eating mine. "Edisson, you will eat yours when you come back." She responded.

To make a long story short, I was not happy with that decision and apparently she could see that on my face upon returning from delivering that meal while eating. Subsequently, she said, "Son, if I had waited for you to finish eating your dinner, that family's meal would have been cold, which could have been interpreted as if we had sent them a leftover food." "Mom, it was not leftover." I replied. "You and I knew that was not leftover, but they did not; therefore, it was necessary for them to receive it while it was warm." She explained. Bear in mind that there was no microwave at that time to warm foods. Looking back while examining the situation, I have concluded that my mom was right.

Instilling Values

Looking back, I realized that my dad intended to instill some responsibility in me because he assigned me to go to local companies, monthly, to pay electric, water, and telephone bills. I learned quickly to report to him with receipts after paying them, "Son, reporting to someone after a mission is accomplished is a sign of accountability and discipline. If practiced consistently, it may become a crucial life skill."

My dad was on time everywhere he went especially for work or church. He was, indeed, a real military person in terms of discipline and time management when it came to his daily routine. One day, he realized he was going to be late for a 2:00 – 10:00 PM work shift and he left without eating dinner. About one hour later, my mom asked me to take the dinner to his workplace, CONASA.

Upon arriving there, he asked me if I already ate because he would like to share his food with me. Yes, my mom made sure I ate before I left. After he finished eating, I was about to leave when he asked if I could stay longer to chat.

Minutes into our conversation, he reminded me how lucky I was as the youngest to have many older siblings who love me. "So, you do not need to stay in school because as the baby of the family they will take care of you very well," he stated.

"Really!" I replied with a big smile and excitement on my face. "My son, I was just pulling your leg to see your reaction," he stated.

Then, he explained, "Do not **EVER, EVER** depend on your brothers, sisters, relatives, or anybody for anything in life! They, too, will have their own problems to take care of. If you were to ask them for something, and they refuse, it is not because they do not love you."

He continued by saying, "they must provide for their own families first before they can offer a helping hand if they wish, but not out of obligation. That is a natural law. You should always take

34

care of those closest to your heart before offering a helping hand to others."

Then, he added, "If, however, one of them were to give you some money or a gift, take it even if you do not need it and then share it with someone you know who might be in need. Not accepting the gesture could display a level of pride and God does not like people who are arrogant, "The LORD hates all those who have proud hearts. You can be sure that they will be punished."[5]

I will forever remember that father-and-son precious, one-on-one, moment when I was thirteen or fourteen years old. I plan to pass on that valuable life lesson to my three boys. Over three decades later, I was honored to preach at his homegoing service on Saturday, December 6, 2008, and shared that testimony.

Middle School, Condom, and Macho Man

After living in a family bubble for four years, it was time to enter the real world as a kindergartener. The childhood honeymoon was over, and the family bubble had burst. As a result, I began to deal with the real world starting with my classmates.

The first year was the hardest. I experienced homesickness even though I was away for only six hours. As a young boy those hours seemed exceedingly long, and I could not wait for my parents to pick me up. For a while, my favorite parts of school were recess, eating lunch, and when the school day ended.

It did not take me long to start making some friends, playing at recess, and becoming so busy I occasionally did not finish lunch. There were times I did not want to go home when my older siblings would come to pick me up. In fact, I had wanted to hang out with my new friends whose parents were late picking them up.

---

[5] Proverbs 16:5, NIV

A new relationship or friendship seemed to come with new challenges and some bargaining skills. As a young boy, I had found myself doing all those things in elementary and middle school. Friendships were built, as well as rivals in that brief period of time. There were times negotiations had taken place, which in many cases involved the sharing of one's lunch in order to achieve a goal or to be friendly with another friend.

It did not take me long to learn that friendship, sometimes, comes with peer pressure. At the beginning of middle school, one classmate brought a bag full of condoms in his school bag and started giving them out during recess. One was given to me. In my innocent mind, I opened mine and was about to inflate it, thinking it was a balloon to play with. Quickly, one of the boys stopped me and hoped none of the teachers saw what was going on.

As a result, I was pulled aside to be educated about the use of condoms and another one was given to me. Then, I told them that I did not want any because I thought it was something with which I could play. One of the boys, who seemed to have more experience, intervened and said, "My friend, having a condom in your pocket constantly is a sign of being a macho man. Do you want to be a macho man?"

One day later, I was called into a family meeting to be questioned about something one of my sisters had found while washing my school uniform. "How long have you been sexually active?" one of my siblings asked. I inquired about what that meant. "Do not pretend you do not know what it means because we have found a condom in your school uniform," another one interjected.

It was one of the most awkward moments in my life. I was speechless and scared. During the interrogation, my parents did not say anything. I had felt like I had committed a crime. I sat listening to them debating about the condom. Suddenly, my father told everyone to give me a chance to explain my side of that story.

With my trembling voice, I explained everything that happened at school with my friends and the condom. For whatever reason, some of my siblings still did not believe me and kept pressing me to tell them the real truth. "Listen, everybody!" my dad interrupted, and he continued by saying, "I believe my son's version of what happened, I want you all to leave him alone, and throw away that condom."

After listening to my father's verdict, I felt liberated. I thought I was going to be disciplined and probably experience some corporal punishment for something I had absolutely no knowledge on how to use. Looking back, it was a good feeling to witness my father's trust in me.

"Peer pressure is the direct influence on people by peers, or the effect on an individual who is encouraged and wants to follow their peers by changing their attitudes, values or behaviors to conform to those of the influencing group or individual."[6]

There are times some people use peer or social pressure as a way to influence another person to take a particular course of action with a hidden agenda, to achieve a personal goal. About twenty years after experiencing my first round of peer pressure, with the condom experience, I went to a car dealership to buy a used but reliable vehicle before I started my chaplain residency.

After telling the agent the kind of vehicle I was here to buy, he then asked me what kind of work I did. I told him that I was about to start a residency as a chaplain with a local hospital.

Suddenly he stated, "Sir, I think you should buy a brand-new vehicle because you would look bad when you see your colleagues driving some nice automobiles." I thanked him for thinking about my professional esteem vis-à-vis my colleagues but responded that I had to live within my budget. He proceeded with a counter

---

[6] https://bit.ly/3JcnEEm - Access date: 3.23.2021

argument hoping to convince me to go beyond my limited income. After listening to him, patiently, I thanked him for his time and left. I felt like I was being pressured by using my professional entourage to boost my ego.

After examining those situations and my experiences over the years, I am inclined to conclude that peer pressure is a social phenomenon that has the potential to cause minor and/or major personal, familial, and professional damages if not kept in check. Some, however, tend to assume that only young children experience peer pressure and adults are immune to it. It is my understanding that anybody can experience group or social pressure at any age in life.

Case in point, I read a story about a particular wife who asked her devoted and hard-working husband to buy her the latest stove on the market. The husband was happy about the idea. Days later, he told some of his friends that his wife is planning on cooking some interesting recipes because she asked him to buy a brand-new stove.

Weeks later, the husband realized that his wife never used the new stove. She just passed through the kitchen. When he asked her why she wanted the stove, she said that that one of her friends had one and she wanted one, too.

Based on my experience and observation, belonging to any social group carries a certain level of pressure, directly or indirectly. One has to have a balanced self-esteem, a certain level of self-confidence, proactive mentality, and a spirit of discernment to avoid falling into any group trap that could lead to the pressure of blending in or having a sense of social belonging.

Being Afraid and Fearing

As I mentioned earlier, the high school had a marching band. I was thrilled when I was informed I made the list to join it. It was important back then and being a band member was like an opportunity of a lifetime. Members of the school band were popular, and I was one of them.

I started learning to play saxophone, and months later I switched to trumpet with the conductor's blessing because I was fascinated by those three valves and how to learn to play the music solfège from those valves.

The only time marching band students were allowed to use those instruments was during practice, which happened during weekends and sometimes weekdays if we had to prepare for an event. Therefore, practicing at home with a personal instrument was not an option because as far as I can remember, none of us had the opportunity to own a musical instrument. According to the band policy, musicians were not allowed to take instruments home.

The band master encouraged those of us who were learning to play wind instruments, such as a trumpet, to keep working on our lips by whistling, which he believed was better than nothing as we could not practice at home with an instrument.

One afternoon, I was sitting in my parents' backyard with a music sheet in front of me and whistling the notes over and over while pretending to hold a trump and touching those imaginary valves to match the notes. I repeated the process slowly countless times, while increasing my speed and it was a good feeling.

Unfortunately, one day that feeling did not last long because as soon as I realized my father was standing behind me I stopped the whistling, because I had been told children were not allowed to whistle in their parents' presence because it was considered a sign of disrespect. "Why did you stop?" he inquired. "I know I am not supposed to whistle in your presence, and that was the reason I stopped when I saw you."

My dad had a way of using mundane situations to instill valuable life lessons. He told me how much he appreciated the fact I quit whistling when I saw him. However, he explained that could mean I was afraid of him. "Son, I do not want you to be afraid of me. My hope is for you is to develop a level of fear or respect for God and your parents." "What is the difference?" I asked.

In Proverbs 9:10, we have been reminded, "The fear of the LORD is the beginning of wisdom, and knowledge of the Holy One is understanding."[7]

Also, he added, "Having a fear for a higher being and humans will help people to be consistent with their behavior no matter where they are and who is around them. Being afraid of someone, however, may lead to a life of double standard, in which your behavior will be based on who is around or watching you." I thanked him for his explanation and told him that I would do my best to remember the difference.

Dating and Leadership with Challenges

When it came to dating, I never had interest in girls in my classroom. My fascination was to date girls who were in higher grades than me as a challenge to try to keep up with them, intellectually. For what it was worth, I was attracted to those girls, and some of the girls in my class did not like that about me.

Months after starting my high school senior years, the school chaplain, Reverend Fritz Jules, unexpectedly requested my presence at the end of my final class in his office via a written note. Was I in trouble? Did I do something wrong? My heart started racing and could no longer focus during my remaining classes. My mind kept wondering about many scenarios. Being a teenager and

---

[7] Proverbs 9:10, NIV

dating during high school, I thought a girl had gone to him and shared how I broke her heart.

Anyway, upon arriving in his office, he invited me to sit down. I stood because I was apprehensive about what was to come and did not want to be in a comfortable position. I was in a defensive mood, to say the least.

"Edisson, I am going to be out of town for three weeks and I would like you to be in charge of leading the school daily devotion and chapel services on Sundays while I am away." Maybe because he knew what my answer was going to be, he added, "I would encourage you to think about it and let me know your decision tomorrow morning."

Unfortunately, I did not yield to his suggestion and without thinking about it, I turned him down. "Remember, I urged you to think about it!" he reminded me. "I did think about it, sir, and that was the reason I told you I could not do it," I replied, and left his office.

After school dismissal, I went home and, in the evening, shared what happened with my parents, and my dad asked me if I had prayed about the answer before saying no to the chaplain. "No," I replied. He urged me to do so and encouraged me not to say no when situations like these arose because they would help me to discover my social talents and skills. My dad had a way of challenging us without making us feel like we were being challenged.

The next day, I went to the chaplain's office and as soon as he saw me he invited me in and said, "I was expecting you. For a particular reason, I felt in my spirit you would come back with an affirmative answer this morning." We both laughed and I told him that I was up for the challenge.

To make a long story short, it was a remarkable experience in my life as a teenager. During his three weeks of absence, I invited two staff members to preach during chapel service on Sundays and I preached one time.

It was amazing to have the school administration, principal's office, teachers, and the student body supporting me. I will always be grateful for their encouragement.

Upon chaplain Jules' return, I went to his office to give him a report and he said, "Edisson, I already received impressive reports from the school administration, the principal, staff, teachers, and students about your administrative leadership during my absence." I expressed my gratitude to him for believing in me and also for choosing me even though at first I felt inadequate. He, then, asked if I would be willing to assist him for my remaining two years.

Being the chaplain's assistant was and still is one of the great leadership opportunities and experiences in my life. We had a wonderful time working together as a team during those two years. He was a great teacher and a patient man. I learned some great administrative and leadership skills that have impacted my life positively. As a result, I consider him as my first professional mentor.

About one decade later while examining my life as a professional chaplain, I called and asked that chaplain if he could tell me his reason for choosing me among all other students to lead the chaplaincy department for three weeks and then requesting for me to be his assistant.

"I wish I had an answer for your question. One thing I can tell is that happened three times in my chaplaincy career and all those men are now in ministry." He continued by adding, "Edisson, certain things in life will forever remain a mystery. We just need to accept them." As we concluded our conversation, I thanked him for his wisdom and humility.

The French School System

In the French school system at that time, high school students must take and pass two government exams, Baccalaureate one and two, before one can apply and attend a university. Both exams are really tough. The English equivalent is the Scholastic Assessment Test (SAT), in the United States school system, that assesses students' readiness for college. Without the required SAT score, pupils can only attend community colleges like in the French system.

Some students have had to take those exams more than once. If, however, one almost achieves the minimum score, a retesting is available one month later. Without the second exam, one can only attend a community college to learn a trade.

In 1996, I almost failed the first government exam. Therefore, I was one of those students to retake it. My dad had a long talk with me. He encouraged me to put in all my best efforts to pass it next month as it would be an embarrassment for me, and it would have a negative impact on my academic dream. With some extra effort, I passed the second round.

Soon after the new school year began, I received a note from the school principal and chaplain requesting my presence before I left campus. They asked me to build a provisional committee to organize elections for each class from sixth to twelfth grade and wanted me to be president for the executive one.

After listening to them, I explained how I almost failed the first government exam and wanted to focus fully on my schoolwork to avoid repeating the same mistake. I accepted the first two challenges and agreed to form a provisional committee and organize elections for all those classes. I respectfully declined the position of student body president. They thanked me and said that they respected my decision and agreed with me. Fast-forward, over two decades later, I became the president of that same high school first formal alumni foundation, College Pratique du Nord Alumni Foundation (CPNAF).

Again, after sharing that major challenge with my dad, he prayed with me and advised me to go through the list of all my friends I started my high school years with to choose the most responsible and dependable ones to form that temporary committee. My dad would never engage in any endeavors without praying about it first.

"People you choose to be in your circle will and can determine your success as their leader," he explained. "I hope and pray the Holy spirit will guide you in your selection making during this challenging task." He prayed and gave me a hug and said, "I have no doubt in mind that you will do well in this project."

Within days, I began going through my classmate list, mentally, and started filtering names and writing them down. Most of them accepted the challenge. We worked hard throughout the process, and at the end we celebrated the accomplishment. When everything was over, I thanked everyone for their participation in making this challenge a success because without them it would have been impossible to make it a reality.

About one month later, I was sent home for non-payment of the academic entrance and the first trimester fees. At that time, my parents were going through some financial hardship. That was my first experience being pulled out for school fees during a class session in front of my peers. It was a humiliating situation that crushed my self-esteem.

Every minute matters when preparing for final exams and then college. Missing a whole class could have a tremendous negative impact on my government exams preparations, which ultimately would reflect on my grades.

I headed home to inform my parents. On my way home, I saw a relative who had a great professional relationship with some of the high school leaders. I explained my situation to him with the hope he would talk to the administration to allow me to complete that day.

To my dismay, he did not allow me to finish my thoughts, and he told me, "I cannot help you. I am caring for my children now." He did not even let me say anything else and left me standing. I was speechless, embarrassed, and hurt, to say the least. I stood there for a few minutes frozen.

I took a deep breath and went back to school and asked the administrative assistant to meet with the school administrator. I told him that I had been sent home for non-payment. He did not even let me finish explaining the situation before he rhetorically asked, "Are you serious?"

He continued by saying, "Edisson, you have been investing in this school in diverse ways for the past seven years, and that should have never happened to you. On behalf of the school, will you accept my apology?"

He, subsequently, added, "Now, I want you to write me a letter requesting a scholarship and you will receive a full one for the remainder of the school year." I thanked him for seeing me unexpectedly and for the prospective scholarship. "You deserve more than that!" He exclaimed. Then, he gave me a note to give to the finance department in order for me to resume my classes.

One year later, through a local clergy's connection with a seminary in Belgium's capital, Brussels, I was awarded a young ministerial leadership scholarship to study theology and psychology. The one condition was to give a name of someone either in Belgium or another country in Europe, in case of an emergency.

I considered that last requirement a piece of cake because I had a relative from my mother's side in Belgium who was an Ambassador for the Haitian government. I explained to my mom the situation and she agreed to talk to her nephew on my behalf. To my dismay, he refused to be that contact person even though his wife had responded positively during the initial conversation.

That was a huge disappointment because I was so close to receiving that full scholarship. While reflecting on those experiences with two relatives, I could not help but remember what my dad told me five to seven years prior about not counting on families and relatives for anything because, technically, they owe you nothing in life.

My parents, too, were disheartened by those two separate events. My dad assisted me in processing them and encouraged me not to allow those disappointing circumstances or any setback in life to crush my spirit and determine my future. He reassured me that God may have something better and greater in store for me.

1997 was a tough year. I first experienced the death of my 39-year-old sister, Syllotte, the one who took me to our local church in Milot to be blessed as part of the Christian ritual. It was a very emotional and challenging time in my family, especially for me as she was like a mother figure during my formative years.

It was the first time I witnessed my parents become very emotional through tears. Every child has a hero to look up to. Mine are my parents, especially my dad. It was a heart-breaking scene to watch someone I considered my hero, crying while providing emotional support to his wife, children, and planning the funeral service of his adult daughter who left behind a widower, Jean-Rene with two young children, Jennifer, eight, and Joshua, four.

That sister passed away around my birthday. Therefore, planning a birthday for me, or anyone for that matter, would have been inappropriate and I understood that clearly. To my surprise, my father prayed with me in private and read a Psalm from the Christian Bible that matched my twenty-first birthday.

I had many unfortunate experiences during my final high school year. I was determined not to let them interfere with my academic goal to pass the government exam and graduate. There were about seventy seniors, we were excited and ready to plan our graduation upon the successful completion of the final exam.

The school administration, however, decided to have a graduation ceremony date scheduled prior to the government exam result, without involving the senior committee members in the decision making. Frankly, we all felt like we were being treated like small children.

We call for a meeting with the administration to request the graduation ceremony be afterward when the exams were behind us. Unfortunately, things did not go well. We were told that decision was not debatable; therefore, all seniors must graduate before the government exam. That was the way it had been done for years and they were not going to amend it.

As a result, we all had decided to boycott that year's graduation and challenge the school status quo. That Latin term "*status quo*" literally means *the mess we are in*. When the status quo is not being challenged, people will remain in that mess forever. Some people, regrettably, do not like change and tend to feel threatened by any alteration.

All seniors agreed not to graduate that year and showed the administration that they could not have the senior's graduation without students. It was the first time in that school's history that there was no graduation. One member of the administration was so furious, he told us during a meeting that we would achieve nothing in life, and we were a bunch of losers.

The principal interrupted and said to him, "Sir, you just made a big mistake in your life as a leader when you told those young, talented, and smart students that they would achieve nothing in life, and they were a bunch of losers. I would like you to know that I have been observing those young men and women for years and I guarantee you they will achieve remarkable things in this world."

After listening to that short and yet powerful self-esteem booster speech, we all felt empowered. It was and still is a good feeling when young people hear and know that there are adults who believe that they are on their way for greatness, and they can succeed in life.

Once it was concluded there would be no graduation for that year, the main focus shifted as the countdown began to the school exam and then the government one. The latter one, however, was the most important one and without it the dream to attend a university would not be realized. It was and still is the school's policy, nonetheless, for all seniors to take their exam, too, even though it would not really matter.

Challenging Myths and Superstitions

Mastering French, English, math, physics, and chemistry are crucial in preparing for the final government exam. My notebooks for math, physics, and chemistry were extra neat because they dealt mostly with digits.

About two months prior to the government exam, after a class recess, my physics notebook was nowhere to be found. I asked my classmates and some of them assisted me in looking for it but with no success.

Many things went through my mind. One of them had to do with the level of superstition that existed and still exists in the Haitian culture. For instance, there seems to be mystical explanation for practically everything with the idea someone is wanting to cause harm. The sad part it has been engrained in the culture so deeply and in almost every life's aspect.

There seems to be slight difference in belief among secular and religious or people or faith. For instance, some religious people tend to put more emphasis on praying at 12:00 PM or midnight with the idea that mystical things happen around those times. Those who do not hold this mindset are deemed careless or naïve.

My father, for example, had Parkinson disease for about ten years with his hands trembling only when inactive. He went to several trained medical specialists in Haiti and overseas seeking treatment, and even participated in a medical study in Florida. He transitioned at 84 years old.

Days after the funeral, one religious lady told me, "I heard that your father was given a disease in the form of trembling hands, in CONASA, where he worked for years." How do you know? I asked. "I do not know. That was what I heard," she replied. I used that opportunity to educate her about Parkinson's disease and informed her my grandmother had the same disease in her old age.

The idea that someone wants to harm you, mystically, is unfortunately extremely popular. This type of belief seems to be passing from generation to generation. There is always someone to blame. Nobody has had a natural death. It does not matter if that person was killed by a car accident or a deadly disease or with old age.

Superstition is a cultural phenomenon that can have different meanings to various cultures. In America, for instance, number thirteen is considered unlucky. In China, on the other hand, number four is unlucky. Each culture has its own superstitious beliefs. Superstitions can pass from one generation to the next, intentionally or otherwise. If individuals blindly embrace some superstitious beliefs, they may cause irrational reactions. Therefore, it is healthy to challenge any belief system.

Based on my experiences with the Haitian, Jamaican, and American culture, I have also observed this type of mentality. Many Jamaicans believe in the magical explanation of things as well through Obeah. In the United States of America, however, some people strongly believe in conspiracy theories. There is a magical secret society, illuminati, that chooses heads of states, determines how long people should live, and they have the secret power to reduce the world population through mysterious diseases or pandemics.

During my chaplaincy internship and residency trainings, for instance, it did not take me long while making hospital rounds and visits to observe that there was no room with number thirteen. I was told that it was bad luck to have a room with that number. I have also learned that high story buildings with elevators do not have a button with number thirteen; therefore, there is no thirteenth floor. It is believed that there is always a fire or something bad that takes place there.

My eight-year-old son, for instance, was scheduled to participate in a field day with his elementary class. As the day was approached, he told me that he was concerned about going. Upon inquiring about his sudden lack of enthusiasm, he replied, "Dad, the field day is on Friday the thirteenth and I do not want anything bad to happen on that day." Suddenly, my youngest son voiced his anxiety and said, "I have a medical check-up appointment on that same day and am worried about what kind of sad news my primary physician may share with me." After listening to their concerns, I asked them about the source of their belief. They told me that they watched it on television and heard it at school that something bad usually occurs on that bizarre day and date. I told them that it is a superstition, and every day can be a good day depending on their actions.

My wife and I are intentional when it comes to challenging superstitious beliefs and falsehoods because they may have both negative psychological and behavioral impact on people. We teach our sons to challenge almost everything they watch on television, to listen, and read critically. People who live by fake news or information can be the most dangerous individuals.

With social media, I am always skeptical whenever I receive messages that requested forwarding to an amount of people in order to receive blessings at the end of the day or week. I deliberately never follow through because I tend to consider those requests as superstitious.

There is power in hearing something multiple times and how it might impact someone positively or negatively. The human brain can be misled at times to believe things that do not exist or have no power.

As I was saying about my missing meticulous notebook, I still could not find it at the end of the school dismissal. After pondering the situation from all natural and cultural angles, I decided not to share what happened with my family because I thought that would create some panic in some of them, thinking that someone would try to hurt my academic achievement, supernaturally.

I kept that experience to myself for years. My comforting thought was that my notebook was so neat, and a lazy classmate who did not want to take notes stole it. I finally shared that experience with one of my brothers, Joshua, during the writing of this memoir, and he agreed with me that it could have created a panic in some of our family, knowing our culture.

Bucket List Beyond High School

When it came to what was next after completing the government high school exam, I had different ideas about what I was going to do with my life. Spending about eight years in a juvenile facility and in a death row prison was not on my to-do-list. Also, being in ministry was not (though I was religiously active at home, at school, and in my community) on the list either.

In my mind, being involved in those religious activities was part of practicing my Christian faith. My main goal, however, was to earn a secular degree and later, if time permitted, to study theology as it is the study of God in relationship with people. I am intrigued by how human beings think, their pattern of actions, attitudes, and their display of personality, morals, and character.

I felt confident in my life's road map. I knew exactly what I wanted, when I wanted it, and how I was going to achieve it. As a result, I was ready and determined to do everything within my power to avoid being a minister at an early age in my life.

One of my dreams to attend the Haitian military academy was dashed away while in middle school. In September 1991, a democratic president was overthrown by a military coup d'état, and the military ruled until 1994. The exiled elected president, with the back-up of the United States military, returned, and the army was dismantled.

Within a year, that president introduced a new police force in Haiti. Joining the police academy became a new dream for me and one of my best friends and brothers, Joshua. As a result, we began putting all the requested documents together and increased our daily physical workout in order to be in great shape especially in the area of martial arts.

I must mention that my parents (specially my dad) did not want us to practice karate because he considered it as a dangerous sport where we could break our bones easily, and he and his wife would have to deal with its negative outcomes. We, however, found ways to practice anyway. For instance, we would dress formally as if we were going somewhere important and one of us would carry a bag with our uniforms inside. Other times, we would leave those uniforms at our friends' home to avoid suspicion from our parents.

As we were scheduled to participate in a tournament, we also had to spend extra hours in our dojo practicing for that big sport event. As time drew near for the tournament, our parents declined to sign the authorization slip. Instead, he told us that he knew about our "formal dressing" tricks all along when going to karate training. He, then, added, "You all can participate in that tournament. If you all won trophies, he would happily take pictures with us. However, if one of you end up with anything broken from your body, you would be on your own." To make a long story short, my brother and I did not attend that tournament. As I look back, my parents were extremely protective of us and did not mean that we would be on our own if we were to break a bone.

Anyway, the weekend prior to the official police recruitment, we informed our parents that we were thinking about applying to the police academy. "Are you thinking about it or are you going to apply? Because I have been aware about your plans but decided to say nothing to you all until you inform me," my dad replied. My mom, on the other hand liked the idea.

"Sons, I would strongly urge you to reexamine your decision because dismantling an existing armed force to start a new one would be, eventually, a huge mess and I would never want you to be caught in the middle. That decision, however, is in your hand because you are an adult," he explained.

After the United government brought democracy back into the island, there was supposedly peace and stability almost everywhere. The United Nations took over once the US military left.

Democracy can be a misleading ideology if there is no proper foundation built. The United States government does not seem to have a good track record around the world when it comes to introducing democracy to some countries based on my observation. Chaos tends to follow once their armed forces mission ends. A democracy that has been forced into a society by a foreign power will always be a temporary one.

It appears that some countries can only rule by a populist strong man. Not all countries are meant to hold a democratic government. Hence, illiteracy does not go well with democracy. That is exactly what happened to my country. How can one talk about democracy in a society where the literacy rate is extremely low?

According to Wikipedia, The Haitian Educational System yields the lowest total rate in the education realm of the Western Hemisphere. Haiti's literacy rate of about 61% (64.3% for males and 57.3% for females) is below the 90% average literacy rate for Latin American and Caribbean countries.[8]

In most cases, democracy in any society requires a certain level of literacy in order for its citizens to make sound judgement in

---

[8] https://bit.ly/32A9qMQ - Access date: 3.23.2021

choosing a democratic leader. Otherwise, there will always be anarchy, anger, and level of dissatisfaction within that civil society.

Imposing democracy to an undereducated culture is a recipe for disaster. Educating that population should be the number one priority before introducing any type of ideological democracy.

Formal education with a strong emphasis on literacy and reading comprehension helps people to look at things within context, as life usually is, because things do not take place in a vacuum.

High School Senior

As my days were coming to an end as a high schooler, I found myself thinking more and more about my future. I should have control over what I wanted to do with it. It was all about my will be done and not God's. As the popular cliché says, "The sky was the limit." I was ready to explore and enter into a period of self-discovery, socially, and academically.

I have a passion for learning but not in a classroom setting. The traditional school system is outdated. The one-size-fit-all methodology limits some people's ability to excel. While in high school, I earned a diploma in communication with two specializations in videography/photography and public speaking.

It seemed that things were going as planned. After passing the government high school exam, I enrolled in a government law school, Faculty of Juris, and Economic Science, in my hometown, Cap-Haitien. Studying law helps ones to develop some critical thinking skills. Great lawyers tend to be extremely good with words. As a result, some call them "wordsmiths."

54

Upon completing my freshman year, I began to realize that after becoming a lawyer there was a possibility I might end up in active politics, which concerned me because many Haitian politicians are lawyers. Now, after living in three different countries, Haiti, Jamaica, and the USA, I have also noticed the same pattern regarding politics and law practitioners. Hence, the connection between these two seems evident worldwide.

I completed my first year successfully and began my second year. Out of the blue, one of my high school buddies told me about a Seventh-day Adventist Institution, Northern Caribbean University, Mandeville, Jamaica, that had a good business program. He told me about their business school as he knew business administration was on my post-secondary bucket list.

As weeks were approaching to leave my family, emotions were also high, and as a result, there was a split in the family when it came to letting me go to a foreign land to study.

My mom and some of my sisters argued that it would be a terrible idea to let me go because I was too young and could end up smoking the Jamaican drug, ganja, and messing up my life or being involved with wild women, which could also destroy me, in the long run.

Bear in mind at that time, I was twenty-three years old, and my family thought I was too young. Regrettably, many Haitian parents have a tough time letting their children become independent. There is a helicopter parenting style that causes more damage than good in terms of mental maturity. Based on my observations, some Haitian adults seem to be mentally handicapped when it comes to facing life's challenges and decision making, as a result.

I am still amazed by my father's parenting style when it came to gradual freedom and responsibility into adulthood. My father believed at that age I should know right from wrong and wanted me to go; otherwise, he and his wife had wasted their time instilling in me those Christian and family values.

"Let him go!" My dad stated. He continued by saying, "When he arrives in Jamaica, if he chooses to be involved in smoking ganja, being involved in sexual immorality, and not focusing on his studies, he will have to live with the negative outcomes of his decision for the rest of his life. On the other hand, if he studies hard and becomes successful, he and his future family will be the ones reaping the benefits."

After intensely listening to both sides of the aisle's arguments, I thanked them for sharing their emotional concerns and promised that I would not let them and God down.

My dad had a red leather English Bible he received as a gift from an American missionary and decided to give it to me. Before doing so, he held it in front of me and said, "May this sacred book be your guiding light. I encourage you to read it as you are about to live in an English-speaking country."

Fast-forward, about less than two years later someone from my floor in the dormitory borrowed that Bible without my permission and never returned it. I never told my dad about that missing Bible because he would have been disappointed. Knowing him, he could have said that nobody would have been able to steal it if I was using it.

Chapter Three

Life at a Seventh-day Adventist University

Bound for a Foreign Land!

On Sunday, January 16, 2000, my dream of studying abroad begun, at age twenty-three, on an international flight bound to Curaçao. I left loved ones, relatives, and friends, to go to a foreign land to study. It was a mixed feeling; I was thrilled and yet sad but was ready to start my new my academic chapter.

There was no direct flight from Port-au-Prince, Haiti, to Kingston, Jamaica; therefore, the airplane had to make an overnight stop in Curaçao, a Dutch Caribbean Island. Its official language is Papiamento, that is, a Portuguese-based Creole language.

After going through their immigration custom service, with my limited English, I asked an airport employee where I could find the nearest hotel to spend a night because I had an early flight to Kingston, Jamaica, the next day. To my dismay, he said, "No English!"

Then, he called someone in his native language and that gentleman, thankfully, could speak English. I asked him where I could find an affordable motel to spend a night. He told me that those motels are not near the airport, and it would be better to spend the night at the airport. I thanked both of them and pulled my suitcase to the nearest restaurant in the airport to eat.

Living in a New Culture or Time to Face the Music

The next day, I embarked to my final destination Kingston, Jamaica and arrived safely to Northern Caribbean University (NCU), a Seventh-day Institution, which was about a one hour and thirty-minute drive away. That drive was professional and kind throughout the long trip; and even introduced me to my first Jamaican drink, *Ting*.

Once arrived in the dormitory, I was greeted and welcomed by the manager. Then, he called one of the Haitian students who was already there to take me to my room. Later that day, they gave me a tour of the campus, shared some cultural elements, and some of the "*dos* and *don'ts*" of the dormitory.

The next morning, with the assistance of one of the Haitian students as my interpreter, I was able to fill out some forms, apply for a student identification card, and a cafeteria pass to use during mealtime. That card was loaded with $500 US dollars for a whole semester.

Days later, a professor from the English department requested my presence. He welcomed me to Jamaica and the university. "Edisson, on Monday, January 24, 2000, at 2:13 PM, I would like you to come to my office to take a written English test in order to evaluate your English proficiency," he informed me.

After knocking on his door to make him aware of my presence, he told me that I was late because the appointment was at 2:13 PM and not 2:15. "Anyway! Next time, be on time, sir!" he declared.

Trying to be smart, I told him that my watch was two minutes behind his. He looked at me and said, "I would strongly appreciate if you could set up your watch with that clock on the wall (while pointing it out) to avoid any further misunderstanding with upcoming meetings."

He gave me a five-page written English test and told me I had one hour to complete it. After reviewing my answers, I completed the test in forty minutes. He was impressed and, with a big smile, told me that I was ready to start taking two classes while taking advanced English classes. Before doing so, I had to return to his office the next day at 11:31 AM for an oral exam.

I knocked on his office door exactly at the given time, and he invited me to come in and sit down. We chatted for a few minutes, talking about my wellbeing on campus and my adjustment to a new culture.

"Sir, I would like you tell me about your family, reasons you came to Northern Caribbean University to study Business Administration with minor in Information Technology, and what are your plans subsequently." He asked three simple and yet challenging questions.

I took a deep breath, trying to put my thoughts together, and began telling him about my parents, siblings, aunts, uncles, and cousins. As I was about to move to the next question, he interrupted me and said, "Sir, in the English culture, aunts, uncles, and cousins are not part of the family, they are relatives." I thanked him for clarifying but acknowledged that they are considered family in my country. "I understand, but you are not studying in a French system," he explained and motioned for me to continue.

As I started answering the next question, "reasons you came to Northern Caribbean University to study Business Administration with minor in Information Technology," I ran out of words. I had started itching some places on my body (that I had no business of scratching) just to kill time, while trying to find words.

I was nervous. I had never thought one could be sweating while sitting in an air-conditioned office. I had searched for words but could not find any to continue answering. It felt like it was an eternity but in fact, maybe, less than two minutes had passed.

Finally, he stopped me and said, "I am not surprised by what just happened. I taught English, in Port-au-Prince, Haiti, and Paris, France. Most of my students have always had difficulties expressing themselves, in English, but almost no issues when it came to written exams."

He then said, "Edisson, I am sorry to inform you that you are not ready to start taking classes." I inquired about having an interpreter in class with me. He answered, "that would slow your conversation skill progress" and added "I am giving you one month to improve your English-speaking skills. In the meantime, go to the campus library to keep improving your reading skills and take an advanced grammar class."

One month later, we met, and he asked me the same three previous questions. I answered the first question better but still struggled with details. "How have you been spending your days?" he asked. After answering him, he strongly urged me to spend less time in the dormitory and the library, challenging me to approach people on campus just to strike up a conversation. "Edisson, remember, if you do not practice then your verbal communication skills will never improve. Without practicing, there will be no progress. Let us meet again in one month!" he concluded.

About three weeks later, I had informed him I was ready to meet with him. After answering those three questions, he looked at me and said, "It is obvious someone has been spending less time in the dormitory." Confirming his suspicions, I told him that his suggestions worked.

By communicating with people on campus, I started developing relationships with them. One night, to my surprise, I had a dream in English for the first time. When I explained that phenomenon to my professor, he was pleased and said that dreaming in a foreign language was a good sign, that meant you were immersing into the English system.

That experience helped me to examine the way most high school students in Haiti learn new languages and their methodology. Teachers taught grammar and wrote a list of vocabulary words for students to study, in preparation for the teacher to quiz them. I came to realize that knowing vocabulary meant nothing if those words are not in the context of sentences and paragraphs. Sadly, I have been told that methodology has not been revised.

Anyway, during my first semester on campus, I experienced all kinds of challenges but was determined to advance regardless. One of my biggest challenges was to learn to think like an English person, so that I could communicate effectively. It was hard because the way I learned to structure French sentences was different from English. At first, it was hard, and I even questioned my decision to leave the French academic system.

My relationship with that professor at the communications department grew over time. He shared some cultural tips when it came to grocery shopping. For instance, he suggested that I stop using local supermarkets and buy from local farmers in public markets instead, as those produces are usually fresh and cheaper. "Edisson, this is an effective way to save money. I had to do the same thing when I lived in Paris, France, and Port-au-Prince, Haiti." That was sound advice as an international college student from someone who had previously been in my shoes.

He also encouraged me to fellowship more with Jamaicans who spoke standard English as they would help in improving my communication skills and avoid patois. It was okay to hear and understand the Jamaican Creole, patois, while trying my best not to speak it because it would slow my academic progress.

One day, during a casual conversation, he asked me if I knew the difference between some Jamaicans and some Haitians. I chuckled and told him that there was none because we were all Caribbean.

"Edisson, if some Haitians knew that you had some unexpected money, they would come and share a sad story about the death of a family member or something tragic to have some of that money. On the other hand, some Jamaicans would plot to kill you to take all the money." We both laughed. Looking back, I would say he was more than a professor, he was a mentor. He was well versed in cultural differences, as a product of living in different countries and immersing himself into those cultures.

Ironing and Cooking

When it came to food, the university followed a strict vegetarian diet. If students wanted to consume meats, they went to local restaurants in town and any leftovers had to be thrown away or smuggled carefully on campus with the hope of not being caught by the dormitory manager or any residents' advisors.

Every now and then, the dormitory management team would make unannounced room checks to look for "contraband" (mainly electric stoves, cannabis, and knives). Interestingly, most knives that were seized belonged to students who never cooked. Their knives were kept for personal protection, so they said, but I had never seen so many knives in my life.

Consequently, ours were also seized in the process. We appealed to management telling them that we only used ours for cooking purposes and a deal was made to turn them in to management after each usage.

Cooking was only allowed in the kitchen and the use of personal electric stoves was strictly forbidden and could lead to a written warning or disciplinary actions. The community stove used propane gas and when it ran out, it sometimes took weeks before it was refilled. Even without electric stoves, we found ways to cook in our room. There were times some resident advisors were our lookouts when we used electric stoves, and in return we left some dinner for them.

Eating three meals a day in the cafeteria was expensive and many students would run out of money on their cards by mid-semester. Therefore, we had to be creative in making the card last to final exams as it was more convenient to use the cafeteria than cooking in the dormitory during studies.

About one week before I left my parents' home, one of my aunts, Melanie Bastien, gave me a new electric clothes iron that her son and her daughter-in-law, Mr. and Mrs. Agabus Parvilus had sent her from America. That iron was popular on my floor as many students borrowed it to iron their clothes. Later, that same iron converted into a stove during some challenging times.

We, as Haitians in the dormitory, found a way to cook whenever our electric stove was seized and confiscated. We put the bottom of that electric clothes iron upside down and tied the handle with something (in order for it to remain steady), turned the heat to the highest volume, and put our small pot on it. In no time, the pot was extremely hot and ready to cook. To avoid being caught, we lit several candles behind the door so that the smell would not leave the room. Some Jamaicans who smoked ganjas in their rooms, told us about that trick and it worked.

Before I left Jamaica in January 2006, I gave that electric iron to a Jamaican friend. It is amazing how a gift/blessing can serve multiple purposes and serve others. Over the years, I stayed in touch with that aunt and on Saturday, 12.4.2021, I participated at her homegoing celebration in Miami, Florida.

Looking back, I have learned that blessings should be appreciated, used, and shared with others. I believe that keeping a blessing to oneself without sharing it seems to lose its purpose.

Life on campus was challenging to say the least. Most students have come up with creative ways to make groceries last until the next overseas transfer arrived. Many of us learned how to be creative with Jamaican patties by using two slices of bread with a patty in the middle and it became a sandwich with avocado as a side.

Also, white rice or dumplings with mackerel as well as ramen noodles were the most popular (not because of taste but affordability) meals in the dormitory. Interestingly, two of my former dormmates considered those days as unmemorable and said that they will never eat mackerel and noodles for the rest of their lives.

Anyway, I felt homesick countless times, but my ultimate goal to earn a bachelor's degree kept me moving. Every now and then I re-examined my goal to see if I was on the right track. Evaluating helped me and continues to help me to remain focused with any project I participate in, to keep my eyes on the bigger picture.

Sometimes when discouragement came, one of the songs, *Money,* by the late superstar Haitian singer, Emmanuel Jean-Baptiste, better known as Ti Manno, boosted my determination and kept me going.

In it, he encouraged, "Young men who are studying not ever be discouraged! Do not ever allow money to preoccupy your mind and prevent you from achieving your academic dream. There are several ways for people to make money, but there is only one way to be educated, that is, go to school and study so that you can speak in society. People who have money with no education are limited, and it would be difficult for them to speak like educated people in society. Young men who are studying, do not become discouraged! Your brain is your passport. Money is superfluous."[9]

That song is also applicable for ladies, too, who are studying to achieve a set goal. Learning new skills has never been easy. Education does not make people rich, but it gives them options. Those with limited education tend to have also restricted possibilities in every culture.

---

[9] Personal translation

Cultural Exchange

Speaking of culture, it tends to have different meanings to different people based on one's family and social exposure. Culture is more specific than general. In other words, the word "culture" cannot be used for a whole country. For instance, it seems almost impossible to talk about "the American culture" or any other country's culture. A nation may have a predominant hallmark, but that does not mean it is its general identifier. One may have a general idea about a country's customs or traditions, but that person needs to be cautious not to make a sweeping generalization.

Culture is made of segments, of subcultures, and they have a propensity to alter from communities within each town as well as each family unit of that land. Therefore, it is not fair to put everybody in the same basket.

While studying at that Seventh-day university, I was exposed to several citizens of different countries, mostly in the Caribbean, and it did not take me long to realize that there is no such thing as "Caribbean culture."

Case in point, one day I crossed my legs while sitting on one of the campus benches. "Are you a batty boy?" one lady asked me. "Batty boy? What does that mean?" I asked. "Oh, sorry! It means gay in patois, the Jamaican Creole," she apologized and explained. "What made you think that I was homosexual?" I questioned her. "In Jamaica, only gay men cross their legs like that," she explained. I told her, just for the record, I am not gay and inquired about how I should cross my legs. She told me that heterosexual men usually put one of their legs on top of their thigh closer to their knee cap."

After listening to her, I began to laugh and told her that where I am from people are not supposed to see the bottom of your shoes because they tend to be dirty. Afterward, we shared and compared some other "cultural" lifestyles and customs of both countries, Haiti and Jamaica, to learn together.

Fast-forward, I shared the explanation that student gave me about the leg crossing with some of my friends, in Kingston, two years later and they told me that they had never heard that description. Could it be she learned that from her parents, or some people in her community, and she tried to make it part of the Jamaican culture?

Weeks later, during a moment of fellowship and camaraderie with some Jamaican residents in the dormitory, I showed them some photos of my family from a paper album like some other Haitians did. Bear in mind, smart phones and Google Photos were not invented yet in 2000.

Interestingly, few of the Jamaicans were puzzled by one of the pictures where one of my older brothers and I stood side-by-side with my left hand on his right shoulder. "Batty boy!" one of them shouted. He then said that a man is not supposed to be in a close physical proximity with another man. "For God's sake, he is my biological brother!" I exclaimed. "So what?" he questioned.

Months later, it was rumored on campus that there were two male students in the dormitory who had been spending too much time together and had acted inappropriately. One of the students in question was involved in campus life and chapel activities, he was a religious star leader in the making. He was well spoken, charismatic, and respected.

Unfortunately, those two men were attacked and beaten severely one night after a prayer meeting while all of the residents were in the dormitory. Later, I was told that some of the attackers used construction wood, two by fours, with nails on them, as well as knives to carry out their violent act. Those men were transported to the nearest hospital for medical care.

It was the first time I witnessed such a violent act. I was scared and concerned because of my two previous experiences, vis-à-vis my leg crossing and the picture with my brother. I was ready and prepared to defend myself with my limited martial arts background in the event that I was attacked.

Tensions were high afterward and most of us were shocked by what occurred. The university president came early the next morning to address us, provide support, reassure all resident's safety, and most of all condemn that violent act. It took some time before normalcy resumed.

As I stated earlier, the school has many international students. Oddly, some Jamaicans, students and employees, did not hide sometimes their discrimination against us because of our birthplace. Due to ignorance, they automatically assumed we were vodou practitioners. There were times they would ask us questions about magic. Even though, repeatedly, we told them that not all Haitians practice vodou. However, their level of skepticism was obvious.

One Saturday in the summer of 2000, it was our turn as international students to have lunch with the university president after church. His goal was to build and develop healthy relationships with all international students. To our surprise, he told us that he was aware of how some staff members and students had been discriminating against us based on our country of origin and "magic."

He told us not to be fooled by some of those Seventh-day Adventist students and religious leaders with the "Holier than thou mentality." He then said, "Many of those Jamaicans believe in magic and are superstitious just like most of us Caribbeans, but they try to portray otherwise."

He paused for a minute and added, "When my wife and I, for instance, scheduled to lay the foundation of this house, some of the local church leaders suggested that we slaughter a young lamb and spread its blood on the ground for protection before starting the foundation, which I declined."

He encouraged us not to allow those ridiculous statements to interfere with our academic objectives. "I would like you to know that some of those people just want you to think that they were better than you all. Remember, we are all descendants of slaves." He concluded.

I considered that lunch meeting a self-esteem booster. That university president had a very humble beginning, but he did not allow poverty and people to determine his future. Some of his life's stories were mesmerizing and inspiring. I left his home inspired and thought that if he could make it in life, I would unquestionably succeed, too.

Challenging a System

Though I was involved in church activities almost everywhere I went, I still did not see myself being in ministry. While at NCU, I was active on the campus life and mainly church activities. There was one thing, however, I did not appreciate since I started living on campus. I did not realize that students had to print their names and room numbers in a big notebook every time they went to church as a way to keep track of those who did not attend church. Attending church services was mandatory and I was fine with that, but I was determined to challenge the tracking system.

One day, I told the dormitory's manager that I did not like the church-going tracking system because there should be some level of freedom when it came to attending church since we were all adults. After listening to my grievance, he said, "Edisson, I understand your argument, but I am here to enforce rules. I did not make them. The only thing I can do is to share your concern with my supervisor." He explained. I thanked him and left. Weeks later, the notebook was no longer in the lobby.

Most people, if not all, on campus were deeply religious. They observed their rituals religiously. Based on my estimation seventy-to-eighty percent of students were from the Seventh-day Adventist faith tradition. Many of them would listen to secular songs all week and, by early Friday evening, they would only listen to gospel songs on the Sabbath.

One Saturday evening after Sabbath was over, I was chilling out in front of the lobby and a group of guys said, "we are going to a dance hall club, would you like to come?" and without even thinking about it, I declined.

After they left, I could not help but think about what my parents told me before I left my country, "Son, your life's success is in your hands. Use good judgement before making any decisions!" There were times I was tempted to go, but I thought going to a club would slowly but surely begin to impact my academic dream negatively and as a follower of Jesus Christ that would not be an excellent choice.

Smoking ganja was prohibited on campus, and could lead to school dismissal, but that did not stop some students from smoking it anyway. I became a second or third hand ganja smoker on the street and on campus, but for whatever reason I never had any interest in trying it.

Living on campus could be a blessing or a curse depending on perspective. It could easily be a place for gossiping where some would assess other's behaviors based on their own biases.

Most people there never knew I was of the Christian Baptist tradition because I was active in the church campus activities. Somehow, some of them found out and they came to me to express their disappointment, telling me they hoped and prayed one day I would come to know the truth. I only responded with a smile and said nothing else.

After working as a mail carrier and photocopier technician for two semesters in the schoolwork study program, I was offered a job to work at the vice president's office as one of the information technology persons. My hourly salary was one US dollar because I was an international student and local counterparts paid less. The university president at that time was the product of that schoolwork study program.

Weeks later, the vice president asked if I was interested in helping her care for her small backyard garden. It was the first time in my life that I was exposed to gardening work. She was very meticulous about her garden and wanted me to make sure the flowers were weed free. I would work about two hours and at the end she would give me several bags of groceries. She could not pay me cash as an international student because of the school's policy. Having extra groceries was a blessing, especially during end of semester exams.

As our relationship grew, she gave me half of a scholarship. I was surprised and excited about the news. Later that day, I shared that great news with my fellow Haitians, and some of them shared that happiness while some remained silent.

At the end of the fall semester, the vice president told me that she received several scholarship requests from my compatriots and that they cited my name as the source of that information. I was speechless. She continued to say that she would not want to be portrayed as showing favoritism. Therefore, she would have no choice but to "end it." I was sad and furious with whoever who made that request.

Days later, after pondering the situation, I realized the person I needed to be furious with was myself because I talked too much. I should have kept that blessing to myself. As a result, I learned that sometimes making a blessing public could lead to envy and may cause hatred.

Staying on campus as an international student with no place to go to during holidays was a lonely experience and depressing because the campus was quiet like a ghost town. The Christmas of 2000 was, by far, the saddest one because it was the first time I was away from family and friends during a joyful season.

During the spring of 2001, the university orchestra conductor asked if I was interested in playing trumpet for the orchestra as he was told that I play trumpet. I received half of a scholarship and I joined the orchestra. I only shared that with my family because of my previous experience. Looking back, I was glad I played trumpet in my high school band for seven years.

Life on campus was filled with different activities, one of which was a week of prayer and revival per semester, which usually ended with the ritual of water baptism. I witnessed some students being baptized almost every semester in order to "wash their sins away" as some SDA adherents believe.

Some students came to me and one of them said, "Edisson, do not let this moment pass you by without going into the water to be baptized." I reminded them that I had already been baptized by immersion. "Unless you are baptized in the Seventh-day Adventist tradition, your baptism does not count," one of them practically shouted.

I asked for a Bible and one of them came with a pastor instead. I told them, "The Bible you all, and I, use mentions baptism by immersion once and for all." I reminded them that had been my position and they would not be able to convince me otherwise with a religious tradition.

"Students, Listen! If Edisson had already been baptized by immersion, he cannot be baptized again." that pastor explained to them. That was a victory lap for me! It was a good feeling. Suddenly, all of them became quiet and left me one-by-one.

It was during some studies of the Seventh-day Adventist tradition that I learned baptism by submersion could be done more than once when a sin was committed. I informed the group leader that if that was the case we should be spending the rest of our lives in a baptismal pool because we sin consistently, by our thoughts and actions.

Apparently, they emulate the Jewish tradition of the *tvilah*, baptism, which was used as a means of restoration to a condition of ritual purity. However, water can only clean the human body and not the soul; water baptism is simply an outward ritual.

Then, I reminded him that human beings were not created to live a sinless life because we were born in iniquity; therefore, sin is in our gene. However, our goal is to strive to sin less while we keep our focus on Jesus and stay on the narrow road.

Living a sinless life is humanly impossible, except for Jesus who was both God and a person. Anybody who is portraying to be living a perfect or sinless life must be hiding something. Unfortunately, I never received an invitation back after that encounter.

Life is made up of ups and downs like an electrocardiogram (ECG or EKG) test result. There will be times, you may feel you are closer to God, sometimes, one may even question his or her faith in Him. There will also be plateau moments when you have a sense that nothing is really going on your faith journey. Mountain top or valley experiences should be considered teachable moments for believers in Jesus Christ and not a means to brag or leave the faith.

Based on my observation and experience with the Seventh-day Adventist tradition back home in Haiti, in Jamaica, and in the USA, they seem to be in the Judeo-Christian tradition where one foot is in the Jewish tradition and the other in Christianity.

Even though I was active in the SDA tradition while living on campus, I missed fellowshipping with my theologically like-minded baptists. I was curious about finding a local Baptist church in town and was told there was none.

Finishing the Race

In a race, for whatever reason, some would give up, others would join a different path, and that was the case with some of the Haitians students. As a result, one of the few who stayed wanted to give up, too, and asked for my opinion. I told him that I came to Jamaica on an academic mission, and I was determined to finish it no matter how hard and challenging things were.

Subsequently, we made an academic pledge to support and encourage each other. Fast-forward, in 2004, he attended my graduation in Kingston, and I did likewise for him in Mandeville. Now, he is practicing law in Florida, USA. I have a PhD in Christian Counseling, practicing as a spiritual care counselor, and volunteer as an associate pastor at a local church.

Later, in the spring of 2001, I started that semester and continued working at the vice president's office as an IT person. I was busy with study, work, campus activities, and the orchestra. I was overly excited for the fact that I was on track in achieving my academic dream. I even began thinking about my next plans upon graduation, in the next two years or so. It was a great feeling to have my dreams being unfolded as plans.

Chapter Four

Living with Four Hearing-Impaired, Dream, and Interpretation

One Friday afternoon before sabbath began, I went to downtown Mandeville for grocery shopping and noticed a Mandeville Baptist Church sign. I was puzzled because I was told otherwise by someone on campus.

A week later, I visited that church, and I was spotted as a visitor. At the end of the service, a gentleman who introduced himself as Donville Jones came, and greeted me in Haitian Creole, "Bonjou! Koman ou ye?," meaning, "Good morning! How are you?"

He told me that he and his wife, who was not at church that day, had been to Haiti several times. Then, he invited me to his house and promised to take me back to campus later.

He introduced me to his wife, Phyllis, we chatted for a while, and had lunch together. During our chitchat, I learned that he was the campus manager of a deaf ministry, Caribbean Christian Center for the Deaf (CCCD), in Knockpatrick, Jamaica.

From that day on, a friendship was born. Almost every Sunday, he picked me up on campus for church. As a result, I became deeply religious because I was still going to church on Saturdays to continue learning about the SDA faith tradition.

Weeks later, Mr. Jones offered some financial assistance by allowing me to live in his ultimate retirement home, rent free, in one of the bedrooms where four hearing-impaired gentlemen were already residing. He acknowledged how costly residing on campus could be.

Blessings in Disguise

After sharing that option with my parents, it was time to say goodbye to my friends in the dormitory and join those four deaf men. It did not take me long to question that blessing because verbal communication was not possible.

Subsequently, I became the go-to person in the evening to check their cell phones' remaining money balance and write it on paper, for them to keep track of their usage, because there was no option to check their balance on a phone screen yet. They used their cell phones to text. The most popular phone then was the first Nokia generation.

The worst part of that experience was those evening knocks on my door. Unfortunately, they could not hear how hard they had knocked. I wrote on paper not to knock so hard because it frightened me especially when I was sleeping and encouraged them to be more considerate. Unfortunately, not all of them followed those instructions.

Weeks went by and I still could not communicate with my fellow housemates, I was running out of patience and ideas, becoming frustrated at times. The only time I was able to speak was when the owners, Mr. and Mrs. Donville Jones, would come once a week to lead a Bible study.

They were very faithful in their weekly Bible study rendezvous. We spent months reading and studying the book of Proverbs from the Christian Bible. Due to the fact most of them were intellectually challenged, they used the *English Version for the Deaf* version of the Bible, which also calls, *Easy to Read Version*. In it, they use frequently common words and easy to understand.

Those weekly Bible studies were special, and I thoroughly enjoyed those days as a young man. As a result, I had developed a great interest in the book of Proverbs, which is filled with wisdom for daily living.

Most Caribbean men are passionate about soccer games, and it is considered the most popular sport. By the way, many Haitians have been known as soccer fanatics when it comes to certain international teams. Strangely, the 2002 FIFA World Cup began several weeks after I moved in and those men liked that game, too. There was only one television in the house, and we all had to use it to watch those teams play.

I did not really enjoy that World Cup because those men became excited while watching and their exhilaration level caused them to make noise with their mouths especially when their teams played. To make a long story short, I had to leave them because I could not hear anything from the TV. I reached a point where I was losing patience with them and my attitude toward them was altering slowly, and not in an effective way. Due to my living predicament, I even questioned the blessing of free housing.

After pondering and praying about that dilemma, I decided to change my attitude and began to integrate into their world. I decided to learn sign language because being frustrated would take me nowhere. Hence, I used the challenge as a learning opportunity.

Subsequently, I started spending time and fellowshipping with them even though I understood nothing. Then, I found myself carrying a small notebook around to ask questions about how to communicate certain words through sign language. Remarkably, my feelings toward them improved including my stress level as I began integrating into their world and culture.

As I was about to finish the 2002 spring semester, Mr. Jones asked me about my summer plan. I told him that I intended to take one class but was not sure yet. "Would you like to work at the deaf ministry during that summer, as the account assistant and at the school computer lab?" He asked. "Sir, I would love to, but I do not know sign language." I replied. "Really!" He exclaimed! Continuing to say, "Edisson, I am confused because your housemates told me that you are doing well communicating with them and that was the reason I asked you."

It was an unforgettable experience working mostly with hearing impaired children and adults. That was a summer to remember! Months later, one of those men was getting married and to my surprised he asked me to be master of ceremony at the reception. I felt honored because I did not realize I had such a significant impact on his life, which was the reason he gave for choosing me.

Dream and Interpretation

As time went by, I started having some guilt about ministry. I felt like God was telling me something, especially when I was chosen by a local pastor in my hometown, Cap-Haitian, to receive a young religious leader scholarship to study Theology and Psychology at a university in Belgium. Nevertheless, I pressed on with my study.

One night, after retiring to bed, I dreamed that I was in my hometown driving with no destination in mind. Then, I saw that same pastor calling me to come back to him. I slowed down a little bit and said I would be back, then kept going. "Edisson, don't you hear me calling?" He shouted. I looked back through my rearview mirror and told him to hold on and kept driving. He called me a third time with a much louder voice and said that I needed to stop and come back. I abruptly woke up and felt confused for a minute. It was after 1:00 AM, and that was the end of my sleep that night.

Oddly enough, each time I attempted to fall sleep again, I saw that pastor and he kept asking me to come back. Finally, I went on my knees and asked God for forgiveness for whatever I did wrong (consciously or otherwise) and implored him for guidance.

The next day, I explained the dream to my landlord, Mr. Donville Jones, who was a Baptist deacon at the same Church in Mandeville where I met him. I had also explained to him different plans I had after high school and my experience with that pastor back home, to him.

After listening to me, he strongly urged me to pray and, if possible, fast about the dream. He further encouraged that I spend time in God's presence for wisdom and direction. Before he left, he quoted, "…It is hard for you to kick against the goads."[10]

After weeks of soul searching and seeking God's guidance, I decided to interpret that dream as if God was calling me into ministry. As a result, I stopped pursuing the secular degree and said to God like Isaiah, "Here I am. Send me!"[11] I struggled with the process. I was halfway to my bachelor's degree, and now considering another academic field of study. I was confused. I was not sure if I was making the right decision about quitting that program. I lamented in my room and questioned that dream and the way I was interpreting it.

I never thought God could have called a sinner like me to work with His people. I thought one had to meet some criteria or be equipped before going into ministry. Looking back, I felt like I tried to run away from becoming a clergy several times. I learned that I could run from God, but there was nowhere to hide because He is omnipresent.

To be clear, I had nothing against clergies. In fact, I intended to be in ministry later in life but not so soon. My plan was to be a "good Christian," whatever that is, by following the golden rule.

As I was becoming closer in making that major decision, I wondered about what my parents and sponsors would say after spending two years studying law in Haiti and another two years in the field of business and information technology.

I finally called my family, explained to them what happened, and received mixed reactions. Some expressed their disappointment and accused me of being ambivalent about my academic

---

[10] Acts 9:5, New King James Version (NKJV)
[11] Isaiah 6:8, NIV

pursuit. My father, on the other hand, said that he was not surprised by the ministerial decision.

Consequently, he said that he could see God's hands guiding me into ministry years ago but decided not to say anything because he did not want to influence me. He believed my reactions would have been different.

Then, I looked at different seminaries, but chose Jamaica Theological Seminary (JTS) in Kingston. In the meantime, I notified my boss at the university provost about my plan and would submit my resignation upon receiving my acceptance letter.

She told me that she respected my decision, but expressed disappointment and concern about my school choice in Kingston by asking, "Why don't you apply to our seminary here?" She also implied that she could assist me with a full scholarship. I told her that I already started the process with another seminary, which was in line with my personal religious tradition.

Subsequently, she reminded me that Kingston was an extremely dangerous place, and I could be killed easily. I thanked her for her concern and told her that I believed God would protect me because I was going to Kingston on a mission, and I could be killed anywhere. Then, she said, "Good luck, but remember what I told you about Kingston!" In retrospection, I thought she was upset for the fact I turned her SDA seminary proposal down.

Weeks later, I was interviewed by a lady who was a counseling professor at JTS and days afterward I received my acceptance letter. It was time again to start packing to migrate to Kingston to begin a new life where I knew nobody.

Chapter Five
Life in Kingston, Jamaica

As the time approached to leave Knockpatrick, Manchester, what that university vice president said about Kingston as an unsafe place to live kept echoing in my head. I even questioned my seminary choice. Yet, I was determined to proceed with my plan.

Before leaving, Mr. Jones made arrangement with his chauffeur to drive me there one week before the academic year began in August 2002 as he was scheduled to be in Kingston on business. Mrs. Jones on the other hand sent me with groceries for several weeks.

My hearing-impaired housemates were sad when I informed them of my departure. I, too, became emotional during our last meeting because we developed such a healthy relationship. To my surprise, the deaf ministry organized a farewell party on campus, and all of them had the opportunity to say a few words. They gave me a red cover, *English version for the Deaf Bible* as a souvenir for everything I did for the hearing-impaired community.

On the day of my departure, my adoptive Jamaican parents promised me that they would check on me on a regular basis and would visit me at times. They kept their promises and surprised me countless times with groceries. I am forever grateful to God for their love, hospitality, and friendship. They impacted my life positively and continually do.

After that experience and more on my life's journey, I am inclined to believe that, for better or worse, we do not meet people by accident. Any encounter has a potential to turn into a healthy lifetime relationship or enemy. It is up to those involved to nurture and invest in it.

After examining my relationship with Mr. Donville and his wife, Phyllis Jones, as well as their two daughters (who were studying overseas), I felt like God had sent them into my life for a reason. They went above and beyond to make sure that I was okay while staying in their home. They were more than friends. They had become my adoptive Jamaican parents.

Mr. Jones was and still is my spiritual mentor. I will call him for prayer and wisdom when making major decisions. Mrs. Jones instilled in me some motherly wisdom as a 25-year-old man when it came to choosing a life partner. They both filled with godly wisdom and yet down to earth.

Politics on Campus and Teachable Moment

My first weeks were challenging because I had to learn to re-adjust to a new culture. I hoped that would be the last time I went through that experience. I asked God for strength and courage to remain focused on Him while slowly immersing into the Kingston life on campus.

Everything was going well academically and socially. I was active in the campus life, school politics, and I was elected a member of the student association. I campaigned extremely hard and won that election with a landslide against my Jamaican contender.

Appealing to the students' voters one last time before the
election to come out and vote for the purposeful leader!

Before I knew it, I had that first trimester under my belt, and it was a great feeling. I was determined and hungry to learn. In the meantime, I faced some challenges and was able to overcome them with the support of some incredible professors and students.

One morning, one of the seminarians asked, "Edisson, how was your night?" "Not good!" I replied. "That is good! Have a wonderful day!" He responded with a smile. Later that day, I asked him if he really wanted to know how my night was because I told him my night was not good and your response showed no compassion, which was contrary to your personality. At the end, we both concluded that in most cases asking people about certain questions such as, "How are you? How was your day or night?" are like formalities because many of us tend to walk away after inquiring about their wellbeing.

During my time in Kingston, I had the privilege to attend a Caribbean Religious Summit in which I represented my country, Haiti. The focus was on politics, religion, and socio-cultural. I informed the audience that less than 20% of the Haitian population practice vodou and told them I grew up in a Christian family and had no practical knowledge about vodou.

Afterward, a Christian religious leader said, "Edisson, your presentation was informative but as a Haitian I find it hard to believe that you do not know anything about vodou." With a smile, I asked him as a Jamaican how often he smoked ganja. Suddenly, he became offended and said, "Oh, no! I am a Christian." Really! Because back home through television we were under the impression that all Jamaicans smoke cannabis. I explained. Then, he apologized for his swiping generalization.

Teaching and Graduating

Before I began my senior year, the academic dean, Dr. Dameon Black, asked if I was interested in teaching at the certificate degree level. I declined because I did not want anything to interfere with my final research paper; the seminary had a zero tolerance for students who failed to submit a research document. He urged me to think about it and give him an answer in twenty-four hours.

I wanted to decline that teaching opportunity but looking at my high school experience, when I was asked to be in charge of the chaplaincy department and later became the chaplain assistant, I prayed about that offer, and I agreed. That was an awesome adventure, which I will cherish forever.

Waiting for my name to be called and walking on the stage to receive my bachelor's degree with specialization in Christian Education was amazing. One of my sisters, two family friends, my godmother, my adoptive Jamaican father, and my Haitian friend from the SDA school traveled from Haiti, the USA, and Manchester, to support my milestone. I could not have made it without God's help and my unconditional supporters and cheerleaders. It was a memorable occasion.

I will be forever grateful to God who sent many people in my life to support and challenge me during my journey. I personally knew many of my supporters but some preferred to remain anonymous. To all of them, I say thank you.

Collecting my first degree from the seminary's
president, Dr. Dieumème Noëlliste

Back row from right: My sister, Daniella, me, family friend (like a big brother), retired bank manager and former mayor of my hometown, Aspile Fleurant, and my SDA school friend, Guinx Toussaint

Front row from left: My godmother, Ms. Elizabeth Ellison, and a family friend, Frandy Mompoint

Graduation and Beyond

I faced many challenges in Kingston, but I remained focused as a young man. Those Christian and family values instilled by my family, relatives, and mentors helped me and continue to help me make sound decisions. That did not mean I never fell, but with God's help I never remained on the ground for long.

Anyway, after completing my internship year of teaching, I became a faculty member upon graduating on Friday, June 25, 2004. I was also hired to fill in as the academic dean's administrative assistance for three months during a parental leave absence.

Dr. Black was more like a mentor than a boss during those years. He was patient throughout my tenure and taught me a lot about academic administration "dos and don'ts," and how to be and remain professional while serving others no matter their attitudes. He was knowledgeable and yet humble.

Once that lady returned, I submitted my resignation for both positions with the hope to return home to assess my homeland's social and political situation. President Jean Bertrand Aristide was exiled several months prior for a second time by another coup d'état, and both were allegedly sponsored by the United States government. My desires were also to spend some precious moments with my aging parents.

It was the first occasion since I left my parents' home in January 2000 that I was able to spend some quality time and intentional moments with them. I also used that opportunity to give my mom a break as the primary caregiver since my dad had Parkinson disease and he needed full care. Despite his physical challenge, he was still mentally sharp. He would express his thankfulness for any provided care. We spent some unforgettable ministerial, spiritual, and father-and-son quality time that I would cherish for the rest of my life.

Before I knew it, it was time to return to Jamaica. Thankfully, my old teaching position was still vacant, and I was told to arrive by mid-January of 2005. It was a mixed feeling to leave my parents that time.

While going through the immigration service at the airport, an officer stated, "Welcome back, Lecturer Etienne!" I inquired about how he knew I was a lecturer. He explained, "I was one of your students in the certificate program at JTS." That was a wonderful feeling.

After informing my Jamaican dad of my return, he offered me a position to be the coordinator for the Kingston deaf ministry campus. Consequently, I realized that God was preparing me to minister to the deaf community when I was learning sign language free of charge while sharing a house with those hearing-impaired four gentlemen. Interestingly, I was also able to use my administrative and computer skills at both places of employment, the seminary and the deaf school.

I must confess that though I engaged in those activities, I was secretly searching for a business school in England to apply to a Master of Business Administration (MBA) program because I still wanted to resume studying in that field. Yet, I also began developing deeper interest in theology and ministry. However, I asked God to provide ministerial scholarship if He deemed necessary for me to remain in that field.

With the assistance of my late godmother, Ms. Ellison, from Indianapolis, Indiana, I applied to Christian Theological Seminary that she referred me to in fall 2004. The goal was to request a scholarship in their theological master's degree program because I was determined to climb higher on the educational ladder.

As the campus coordinator, one of my job's descriptions was to coordinate with local and overseas missionaries and made necessary arrangements for them and assign them to different ministerial projects once they arrived on campus.

Time to Migrate, yet Again

In July 2005, some missionaries from Grace Haven Baptist Fellowship, a church from Youngsville, North Carolina (NC) arrived for a week of practical ministry. I was told that they were scheduled to go to Honduras but due to a hurricane scheduled to hit that country decided to go to Kingston, Jamaica, instead to minister to some hearing-impaired children through Vacation Bible School and some building renovation.

Within days, a connection was made between the leader of that group, Reverend Dick Graves and I, and in the evenings, we chatted about almost everything. I shared with him my graduate school desire and my plan to go to Indianapolis, Indiana, in the Spring of 2006 to start a master's degree in theology. He wished me well with my plans, and then mentioned Campbell University as a great Baptist school, that could be another option for me.

As the mission team was wrapping up to leave the island in forty-eight hours, all flights were cancelled due to hurricane Dennis that was scheduled to make landfall; therefore, they were forced to stay longer in Jamaica for almost five days longer.

While waiting for flights to resume, Rev. Graves told me that he spoke with his wife about me and they thought I should at least apply at that Baptist university in North Carolina, and they would provide accommodation and transportation. He even told me that I could live with his family until they found an apartment for me.

Frankly, I did not really know how to make sense of what was happening. I thanked him and his wife for that offer and told him that I would pray and think about it. Once the internet connection was back, I applied to Campbell University Divinity School.

There was a period of confusion because I wanted to be near my godmother to support her as she was becoming less active. On the other hand, based on my research, North Carolina seemed to be more appealing, but I did not technically know anybody there.

After informing my godmother about my decision to go to NC instead of IN, she told me that she respected my choice and would continue to support my academic ambition as long she was able because she believed in a well-trained brain.

Then, she told me that the location did not matter as long as I was being educated. Subsequently, she said, "Son, some church leaders would behave as if they owned you after investing in you either through education or ordination. I hope you would never experience that situation because it could be a disgusting and appalling feeling.

Also, she added, "Most people are selfish by nature; therefore, doing good to someone in need must come from God because He is good. Unfortunately, many pastors are more concerned about their own ministerial ego than giving God the credit for using them as a conduit." I thanked her for sharing her ecclesiastical experiences with me in that context.

Several months went by, I heard nothing from both schools and needed to inform the seminary's academic dean whether or not I would renew my contract. I asked God to let me receive the I-20 from the school he wanted me to attend, first. At that point, I was ready to go to either location.

Less than two weeks later, I received my I-20 to apply for a graduate student visa at the US embassy in Kingston, and days after, the package from the other school arrived. I sent a thank you letter to that school.

Afterward, it was time to start packing once again to face a bigger challenge in a larger country and I was mentally ready for it. I like challenges because they help me to face my weak areas and find the courage to grow. I believe shrinking takes place when there is no growth.

Chapter Six

Dating a Senior Pastor's Daughter

During my undergraduate theological training in Kingston, Jamaica, I lived on campus. One of the things I learned quickly was there would always be gossips when living in a community, and there seemed to be no exception in terms of secular or religious communities.

Our secular society tends to set apart the Christian community when it comes to gossiping. Unfortunately, my experiences with some churches in Haiti, Jamaica, and the USA appeared to be the epicenter of gossiping. Religious people have a way of putting a "concerning spin" into a situation whenever they want to gossip about someone in their religious community.

Prayer meeting seemed to be the place to go, if one wants to know what is going on in other parishioners' lives. I tend to call it "religious or spiritual gossip meeting" instead of prayer meeting. They use religious facilities to gossip in order to not feel bad because they are "requesting prayers for so-and-so" while sharing that person's personal life publicly, without permission.

Galatians 5:22-23, "But the fruit of the Spirit is love, joy, peace, forbearance, kindness, goodness, faithfulness, gentleness and self-control..."[12] For some religious folks, gossiping should have been one of them because they like a good gossip.

There were two ladies supervising some preschoolers at a local church. Within minutes they began gossiping, and as a result, lost focus on their assigned ministry. One of the children wandered away. When someone returned the child, the ladies acknowledged that they should stop gossiping and watch those toddlers.

---

[12] NIV

Dating on Campus

Though living on campus was expensive, there were security officers present all day and night. I liked it because Kingston has been considered one of the most dangerous places in the world, back then. Before I left Jamaica in January 2006, there were over 1,500 people who died brutally according to the 2005 police report.

Life on campus was distinctive because there were more ladies in ministerial training than gentlemen, and many of them were single. Therefore, some people tend to consider college life as a venue to find a life partner, and they will do anything within their power to make that happen.

Months after I started the program, I became friends with a lady who was old enough to be my biological mom. She was a retired teacher and felt the call into Christian ministry. She and her husband had three children. It did not take long to be introduced to her family. As the relationship grew, she considered me like her oldest son.

Over time, she became very protective of me on campus, and some of the ladies were not pleased with that situation. She was fully aware and did not back down. One day, she said, "Son, some people are in theological seminary with their own agenda. Be wise and be vigilant with some of the ladies on campus."

She invited me to her home some weekends to spend time with her family. Later, she expressed her interest for me to be in an emotional relationship with her oldest daughter. I told her that I would rather remain a family friend in order to preserve our friendship. If things were to go wrong between her daughter and me, it would be awkward for us to remain friends. She agreed.

Her husband was a farmer. Almost every weekend, he would bring her fresh produce and a separate bag for me. He took exceptionally diligent care of his family. He reminded me of my biological father and his dedication to his loved ones, duplicating his proactive spirit as a provider.

With the dormitories next to each other, people could smell food whenever someone was cooking. My fried beans with seasoning and rice did not take long to become the most popular dish on campus.

My adoptive mother and I made a deal in which I would prepare rice for a week, and she would provide me with enough meat for a week. My natural homemade juice was also popular. I enjoyed cooking and preparing juice from scratch.

In the meantime, some of the seminarian ladies on campus became furious with my adoptive mother because I rarely fellowshipped with them or invited any of them on a date. Some of them began spreading rumors that I was in an intimate relationship with that lady.

The rumor spread like wildfire. Even the director of student affairs called me into his office to ask about it. He told me that those ladies had not provided evidence of an intimate relationship. I told him that the reason they have not been able to provide him with any proof was because there was none.

At the end of the meeting, he encouraged me to be more inclusive when fellowshipping on campus. I thanked him but told him that I had healthy relationship with everybody on campus but not all would be my friends.

Because most of those ladies were single, it felt like a competition to hunt for a boyfriend. Dating someone was not on my to-do-list. I was academically driven and did not want to be distracted by anything. I was determined to complete my bachelor's degree.

Well, sometimes love comes one's way without looking for it. One late evening, I noticed a young lady, Samantha, sitting alone on one of the benches on campus. I approached her, introduced myself, and asked if she was okay. "Yes, I am waiting for my dad who is in a meeting." She explained.

Then, I offered to keep her company in the meantime. "Sure!" She replied. I stayed with her for almost two hours. She expressed

93

her thanks, and we exchanged phone numbers. Through campus gossip, I learned that she was the oldest daughter of the seminary's board president, and her father was also the senior pastor of a church in town. We stayed in contact for weeks as acquaintances. Later our relationship moved to friendship and graduated to dating. She invited me to the church where her father was pastoring.

During my tenure as a seminarian, I visited countless churches. As a practicing Christian, I am always ready to visit other churches as long they are worshiping God. I am not fussy about worship style because we are different and yet unique in our own genre when it comes theological understanding of doing things.

Little did she know I had visited their church many times before because it was near the seminary. As my relationship grew with the leaders of that church and with her, I engaged in different worship activities. The most prominent one was with the youth department where I became an advisor to the committee.

As Christian Education was my specialization, I was able to complete my internship with them in the education department. Also, I began developing a ministerial relationship with the senior pastor, her father.

Samantha was comfortable enough to tell her mom about our emotional relationship, but not her dad. She, her mother, and I, fellowshipped throughout the courtship. The three of us even went to watch a movie together in a theater. About one year into the emotional courtship, I was thinking and planning to propose to her.

During my final year, I was honored and blessed enough to be asked by the academic dean of the seminary to teach some classes at the certificate level, which allowed me to start earning an income. As a result, Samantha and I decided to open a joint bank account. Both of us would deposit a set percentage from our salaries to start saving for our future plans.

Because I was a foreigner, one of her relatives did not think opening a joint account was a clever idea. She suspected I would wait until that account had a lot of money, withdraw everything, and leave Jamaica for good.

As we were approaching our one-year anniversary in the emotional relationship, I asked her if she would agree to move forward with the courtship if her father still refused to acknowledge the fact that we were dating. "Edisson, I love you and you are a great guy, but I would not be able to proceed with this relationship without my father's blessing," she replied. I thanked her for being honest with me and said nothing else.

Sometimes honesty hurts, but it can also open one's eyes in terms of reality. It is like shock therapy. Nobody likes to hear the truth, but it is, sometimes, the best therapy to bring someone back to reality. Indeed, that truth had brought me into a light bulb moment, which was needed, emotionally.

One of many things I do not like is to waste time and energy, especially emotionally. Life is short and too precious to be in a relationship that might be going nowhere. After pondering over her honest answer, I began planning my exit, which was emotionally painful. Hence, I said to myself that if I am not worth fighting for, it is not worthy of staying in this relationship. Candidly, before that I thought she was the love of my life, but I was wrong.

The sad part of that situation was that her father and I had a great ministerial relationship, but he did not think I was good enough to date his oldest daughter or be her husband. Through church gossip, it was learned that he disparaged me with other colleagues when I was not around.

Still, I said nothing to him even though those people gave me the green light to use their names and details as fact, if and when I intended to confront him. I chose not to because his actions said a lot about his character as a leader, especially a religious one.

When I joined that church, I was warned about his double standard or his hypocritical behaviors when it came to dealing with people. He was a back stabber. Looking back, I was naïve and tricked by his public warmth toward me.

After pondering and praying over the future of that emotional relationship, I informed his daughter that we could no longer date, and I explained the break-up was due to her statement about her father disapproving of our courtship's future. I also informed her not to worry about my part from the bank account we had opened together.

Days later, I met with her mother, informing her of my decision to end the relationship with her daughter. She was shocked, to say the least. Then, out of the blue, she said, "Now, my husband will stop blaming me for your dating our daughter." I was shocked by that assertion. I was tempted to ask her what she meant by that but chose not to because I was not going to do anything about it. I had been teaching myself not to learn things that I would not be using. We hugged and she said, "Edisson, you are a nice young man."

About one year after graduation, I began contemplating going back to school to earn a master's degree in Business Administration (MBA) through a scholarship at a university in England or go deeper with a master's degree in Christian Education or Theology (MTh) or Divinity (MDiv) in a seminary in Indianapolis, IN, or a university in Buies Creek, NC.

I was determined to keep climbing the educational ladder because, after earning that bachelor's degree, I felt like I knew nothing. Through persistence and human resources, God blessed me with the opportunity to attend Campbell University Divinity School in 2006.

Before I left Kingston, however, I informed Samantha and her parents on separate occasions that I was going to the United States for graduate studies. My dating philosophy has been, as much as it depends on me, to be civil with any ladies that I dated as well as their loved ones, but it does not work sometimes.

As I stated earlier, I was active in that local church volunteering within the youth department and any other worship services. During my tenure, that lady's father never mentioned anything about linking me with his university connection abroad for a possibility of a graduate school degree. To my surprise, after mentioning to him that I was going overseas to study, he suddenly stated that he could connect me with a school in the USA for a scholarship. I thanked him for thinking about me but declined the offer.

In the meantime, Samantha went to Asia as a missionary, and we still communicated. One day, she told me, "Edisson, my father would like you to know that he is ready to talk to you about our emotional relationship and the possibility for us to resume dating." "Really!" I exclaimed. "Do me a favor, tell your father thank you for letting me know, and I will inform him when I am ready."

Fast-forward, three years later, I went back to Jamaica, as a newlywed for our honeymoon. My wife, Nelcie, chose Jamaica because she wanted to travel the island during our trip. I knew Jamaica better than my own country, Haiti, after living there six years.

During our honeymoon, our adoptive Jamaican parents lent us a vehicle to travel in the island. We visited five parishes, and we went to that same church where I dated that senior pastor's oldest daughter. With my wife's permission, of course, we decided to go to that same church on a Sunday.

While dating my wife, I told her about some wonderful people I had met in Jamaica and how they positively impacted my life. I also shared with her my courtship of the daughter of that church's senior pastor, and she was fine going to that church for a worship service while in town.

I was able to meet the senior pastor in his church office twenty-four hours prior and introduce him to my wife. He told my wife how great I was as a ministerial colleague. Then, I left them talking while I went to greet other staff members.

As we departed, my wife told me she was uncomfortable when Samantha's father began asking her about her profession as a trained pediatrician and wanted to know how much money she made yearly in Haiti, which she deliberately did not answer.

Brain Freeze and Chitchat

The next day, we arrived at least thirty minutes before the worship service started. The reception was beyond my expectation. Parishioners were thrilled to see us. It was like a short family reunion. Young and older people shared how much they missed my presence in the congregation.

Twenty-to-thirty minutes after the worship service began, it was time to welcome visitors then greet one another for a brief fellowship. Well! Well! Well! The senior pastor began by saying, "We have someone visiting this morning with his wife. Hen…, what is his name, again?"

Unexpectedly, our eyes bumped into each other, I smiled, and said nothing. Then, one member stood up and shouted, "Pastor, are you serious? His name is Edisson. He was here with us." He thanked that member. He asked us to stand and almost the whole church acknowledged our presence by clapping.

At the end of the service, those who did not have the chance to greet us, before the service started, came to do so. As I told my wife about Samantha and her mother, we went to both and greeted them. She congratulated us and left immediately. As her mother started talking to my wife, I was told that one of the elderly ladies would like to see me; she was extremely excited to see me after so many years. She thought she was not going to see me ever again before she died.

As my wife and I were heading to another parish to visit one of my Seventh-day Adventist colleagues and his family, she talked to me about the senior pastor's behavior at the pulpit when he could not remember my name. She concluded, "It took me by surprise because the day before while in his office, he called you by your name, and 24-hours later could not remember it. Now I completely believed everything you told me about him. That was odd!" We tried to process the whole situation again in the car while trying to make sense of it. We laughed and I told her maybe he has had a brain freeze and was in shock mode because that could have been his daughter sitting next to me.

My wife said, "Your ex-girlfriend's mother really loved you and missed you." "What do you mean? How do you know?" I asked. "When you left me with her to go and see that senior lady and some other people, she told me how much she loved you, missed you, and said to me to take diligent care of you because you are a good man."

Looking back, it was a wise decision to be transparent with my wife about that previous relationship before I met her because those things could have taken her by surprise. I am glad I trusted my instinct. Also, it was a good feeling, at that time, to visit that church with my wife even though, after examining what happened, I felt bad.

Years later, the senior pastor retired and migrated overseas, but even to this day, I still have a healthy relationship with the leadership of that church in Kingston, Jamaica. I like staying in touch with people I have encountered in my life's journey. I am not a major fan of burning bridges once across them because, one may need to use it again for oneself or someone else.

Choosing a Life Partner

Based on my personal experience and my observation among fathers and their daughters, especially oldest ones when it comes to dating, some fathers seem to have a mental description of a gentleman for their firstborn girls that does not exist. No male is ever good enough to gain their blessing. Without realizing it, the invisible clock is ticking for their daughters in the meantime.

Some ladies seem to be picky choosing a life partner; some like tall guys, others prefer light skin. On the contrary, there are those who are fascinated by dark brown. Still, others focus their full attention on a particular culture thinking that they can only find a good man from a set custom.

As a result, many of them end up spending the rest of their lives alone and sometimes miserable. It has been said that humans have two choices in life when it comes to choosing a soulmate. You can be married and wish you were dead, or you can remain single and be miserable forever.

In many cases, some of them ended up married during the eleventh hour with someone they would have never been involved with if it were not of their emotional clock deadline approaching midnight. Hence, their emotional regrets list tends to be long and filled with remorse while wasting brain cells thinking and wishing about what could I have.

It has been reported that the late American journalist, Fulton Oursler said, "Many of us crucify ourselves between two thieves: regret for the past and fear of the future." There is absolutely nothing you can do about your emotional past mistakes. The only possible thing to do is to learn from them if it is not too late. Remember, it is a mistake not to learn from one's mistakes. Take time to learn from them even with tears in your eyes because they will make you better rather than bitter.

Ladies, you will never be able to please your parents, especially your dad, when it comes to choosing your life partner. You, however, can hear their concerns but at the end of the day the buck stops with you. After all, it is your life and your mistakes if things do not work out.

The sad truth is that statistics are not in your parents' favor in terms of who might die first. It is highly possible they will leave this earth before you. Yes, children, too, can go before their parents as well, but this kind of sudden death is rare, and it is an exception. Hence, in most cases, they have already lived their emotional lives and now it is your turn to live yours with whoever you wish.

Some parents like to interfere in their children's emotional decision even though they did not want their own parents to do the same thing. On the other hand, there are those who want to amend their emotional mistakes on their offspring by behaving like emotional relationship experts without taking into consideration the generational shift.

For instance, I witnessed a comparable situation in my family of origin between my dad and one of my sisters regarding a gentleman she was dating who, originally from out of town, was working in our hometown, Cap-Haitien. My father opposed their emotional relationship on the premise that he knew nothing about that man and as far as he was concerned, he could have been married and had left a wife and children back where he came from. That led to a heated debate between my sister and our dad. She was adamant about marrying that man. She even told our dad, "As a head, you have no choice but to accept whatever hat I put on yours. That decision is mine and not yours."

To make a long story short, my sister and I traveled to that man's province, met his parents, talked to people in his neighborhood, and reported to our parents. I really admire that sister's steadfastness when it came to her emotional life. At the end, she and her husband are married with children and living happily ever after.

While reflecting on that situation, I felt like I was a private investigator in that man's town and neighborhood. I wanted to support my sister in her love quest, after talking to our dad, so we embarked on that across country trip to ease my dad's skepticism, which was understandable as a father.

Many daughters like pleasing their parents, especially their dad. Be aware of that attitude because it may lead to resentment later, which eventually causes deterioration in a family.

Gentlemen, everything I just mentioned is applicable to many of you, too, except the pregnancy and the birthing part. Men can impregnate at any age unless there are some medical circumstances, but the physical energy level is decreasing in terms of being active in a child's life. If, however, financially stable and responsible, the earlier is the better because your children will need your physical stamina when it comes building lasting memories.

Some of you are mommy's boys and your desire is to find a perfect lady of your mom's choosing. Guess what? You will never be able to satisfy your mom's mental list as well. Ladies and gentlemen, do your best to remember that your life, your decision, and your challenges are yours when they come; therefore, do not let anybody dictate your emotional decision when it comes to choosing a life partner!

Some parents do not want their children (especially their daughters) to date in their teens or early twenties without a given explanation. Sarcastically, however, those same parents would tell their daughters, directly or otherwise, who are in their thirties that they would like to be grandparents and wanted to know what they are waiting for to get married. Candidly, it seems like a parental bipolar behavior or mixed messages. Regrettably, many ladies and gentlemen find themselves marrying at the eleventh hour with people they would have never been involved with emotionally.

Chapter Seven
Coming to America

After receiving the necessary documentation for a prospective international student from Campbell University Divinity School, I submitted my resignation letter to JTS and CCCD. No one will ever know how much stuff they have accumulated over the years until it is time to move to a new house or relocate to a different country. I gave most of my possessions away because I could not travel with them.

I had mixed feelings leaving my adoptive country, Jamaica, and many people who impacted my life one way or another after six years. Nevertheless, I was ready and determined to go deeper into the academic world because my goal was to become a universal citizen through higher education.

Before leaving the island, my US host family warned me to dress accordingly because it would be the middle of winter when I arrived. It did not take me long to realize that I would not find winter clothes anywhere in Kingston. Therefore, I waited until I arrived in Florida to buy some as I planned to visit some of my siblings I had not seen in years.

One of my brothers, Joshua, whom we last saw in 1997, purchased my airfare in such a way that I could spend two days with them. It was time well spent reconnecting and fellowshipping even though it was short. One of my sisters, Dieudonne, took me shopping to buy winter clothes. Again, we could not find any, not even a winter jacket. It suddenly dawned on us that Florida and the Caribbean have similar weather and no winter clothes in stores.

I usually do my best to be on time, and sometimes even arrive early, everywhere I am scheduled to go. Consequently, I informed my volunteer ride twice that I wanted to arrive at the Miami International Airport three hours prior to my scheduled flight because I did not want to be in a rush, and he reassured me not to worry and promised me I was not going to miss my flight. Unfortunately, that was not the case. I was given two options: book another flight in two days or go on the plane and have my suitcase sent to my new NC address, I chose the latter.

Unfortunately, some people think that being late is ingrained in people with brown pigmentation. This is a poor argument because most brown people, especially Caribbean ones, would not be late for a job interview or an appointment at an embassy.

Brown people have been associated with that not so good habit and regrettably some other ethnic groups stereotype us with the pattern of tardiness. Case in point, some years ago, two Caucasian Americans from a major political party were talking about a late endorsement and one said to the other that he was running on CP Time, that is, colored people time.

Hypocritically, my people use that term within their community all the time, but usually are offended when it is used by another ethnic group in reference to them. Candidly, sometimes when some people are offended by something it could be because there might be some truth in it. As it is said in Haitian Creole that "truth hurts." I think instead of being offended, we should make some intentional effort to reduce and eventually erase that sweeping generalization. It has been documented that the phrase CP Time or CPT has been in use since 1912.[13]

Anyway, I choose the latter option because I was determined to start my graduate school chapter on time. I never liked to miss the first day of school because I would feel left behind. I might have been the last passenger to board that plane. I was not happy with that person but there was nothing I could do about it except to decline if he were to offer a ride next time.

Before the flight, I put on an extra layer of clothes that I kept in my carry-on to wear before landing, and I used the aircraft

---

[13] https://bit.ly/33MQhaN - Accessed date: 8.10.2021

lavatory to add them. I was uncomfortable but felt warm. I arrived at Raleigh-Durham International Airport (RDU) on Monday, January 16, 2006, which was a holiday commemorating the birth of Martin Luther King Junior, the most influential American leader in the Civil Rights movement. Once I stepped out, I was greeted by the frigid air even with those extra clothes and a suit on top.

I received a warm welcome at the visitor's launch. I was amazed by the number of people who came from Grace Haven Baptist Fellowship to meet me, and many of them were not even part of the Kingston mission trip. Their presence made me feel at home and welcomed in their midst. I thanked them for their warm-hearted reception.

As my luggage was left behind, I had no personal products to use nor any clothes to wear. We stopped by a store on our way home to solve the first part of my dilemma. Pastor Graves told me he would need to make some phone calls to some of his congregants about regular and winter clothes. We also stopped at Staples to buy some school supplies as the 2006 spring semester started the next day, Tuesday, January 17th. I was exhausted, but buying those things felt like I was equipping myself with the needed academic ammunition.

Finally, on our way home, their youngest son Charlie, told me that he was excited because we were going to be roommates. I told him I felt the same way, too, and thanked him for his willingness to share his room with me. "It is my pleasure!" He replied.

I received another warm welcome from Mrs. Ginger Graves and their second daughter, Betsy; the oldest daughter, Shelley, was already in college. A warm and delicious meal was served. Afterward, Charlie gave me a quick tour of the house, particularly our shared bedroom.

Then, in no time, regular clothes and winter jackets arrived as a result of the Graves contacting some males of my stature in their congregation. I was extremely grateful to all of them and, about a week later, my suitcase was finally delivered.

It did not take me long to truly feel like a member of the family. In less than no time, Betsy and Charlie behaved like the younger siblings I never had. They played an integral part in the acculturation process. Moreover, Betsy became my personal stylist by choosing my clothes every weekend for school. She wanted to make sure that her older brother always looked good, and everything coordinated accordingly. She took immense joy in doing it, and I expressed my thanks to her regularly. I must admit that as a teenager she was pretty stylish.

One day during a moment of fellowship, I told her that if and when I married that I would like to have seven children. She told me that in this day and age, most women would not want to have many children. Hence, raising children is expensive in this country and she told me, "For your age you should have started already." I was thirty-two years old. Fast-forward, as a father of three boys I must confess that she was right about the cost of raising children.

About four years later, as my little sister she approved my chosen engagement ring, and was instrumental in assisting my wife-to-be, Nelcie, in preparing for our wedding day. She welcomed her the same way she did for me. Based on my experience, Betsy has never met a stranger.

As a big brother, I am impressed by her academic accomplishment after graduating from Meredith College with a Bachelor of Arts in Dance Education in 2012 and beginning her teaching career at Broughton High School in January 2013 as the director of Dance. She was named Wake County Teacher of the Year 2017-2018 and became the National Magnet Regional Teacher of the Year the following academic year 2018-2019. She is a loving person, passionate dancer, and caring teacher.

My coming to America was an interesting experience apart from those hiccups with my airport ride. I would never forget that frigid air I felt at the RDU airport because as a Caribbean person that was brutal.

Less than a month later, I went skiing in Sugar Mountain Resort with young people during a weekend church retreat. It was the first time I experienced snow and it was both experimental and brutally cold. During that trip, I was literally baptized by snow.

Chapter Eight
Graduate School and Sugar Mama

The next morning, pastor Graves chauffeured me to Campbell University Divinity School, which was an hour and twenty-minute drive. We had to wake up at 5:30 AM to avoid the rush hour because my first class, Introduction to Theological Education, began at 8:00 AM.

At the end of my day, I felt exhausted and overwhelmed. Things happened so fast between the time I arrived in NC and the beginning of my graduate journey. I felt like I was on a mission, and there was no time to waste.

Within weeks, once again, I experienced another cultural shock. This one had to do with being my first time living in a big country, being exposed to a different ethnic group and culture, living in a different setting, and worshipping God in a Caucasian congregation. I found myself being extremely careful because I did not want to do or say anything that would be inappropriate or offensive in that unfamiliar environment. I did not want to offend anybody. I did the same thing in Jamaica, but I was not as cautious as I was here because Jamaica and Haiti have a common denominator, the ethnicity.

I had enrolled in the Master of Arts of Christian Education (MACE) program. I had fallen in love with Christian education during my tenure teaching at Jamaica Theological seminary maybe because I had received some encouraging feedback from the academic dean office and students.

While experiencing homesickness, I had to learn not only the American and southern culture, but I also had to learn to keep up with the pace in which my professors were teaching; especially after taking a two-year break from being a student.

When it came to spelling, I had to stop using British spelling and begin using the American versions of certain words. I learned to use the American style promptly because some of my professors started marking me down for misspellings. Frankly, at first, I thought those professors were being mean and picky but looking back I realized that learning and unlearning was part of the academic process.

By mid-semester, however, I began developing a great interest in theology. At the end of my first semester, I switched to the Master of Divinity (MDiv) program. My brain was expanding in every sense of the word, culturally and academically. I was learning new ministerial skills while building healthy relationships and friendships with some school staff and my peers.

I had come to realize that learning could be fun and dangerous at the same time. It could be fun if used to impact people's lives positively and make the world a better place. On the other hand, it could also be perilous if used to make people feel inferior especially if they are not as educated as we may think we are. I asked God to help me remain humble and stay in touch with common people as He opened doors for me to learn and climb the educational ladder. I knew that my relationship with people was more important than education.

The first spring semester was under my belt. Summertime had arrived! I was looking forward to it. I began to shed all the heavy clothing.

Nine-year-old Charlie was a wonderful roommate. He assisted me in the culturalization process as well as with the pronunciation of some American words. Fourteen years later, I was honored and humbled to officiate Charlie Grave's religious wedding ceremony to the love of his life, Katheryn Carlton, on Saturday, October 10, 2020. They were determined not to postpone their wedding due to the COVID-19 pandemic because they felt like nothing should come between them and their big day.

My tenure with my host family was great. I felt at home and comfortable, but at the same time, having a personal space was also important. There was a time, for instance, I wanted to stay up late; having a roommate made it impossible to stay up past his bedtime because I had to be considerate.

About three months later, I moved into my studio. It was a great feeling because I had missed my personal space. While studying, some church members helped with meals and groceries while others with transportation as I was going through the process with the Department of Motor Vehicle (DMV) and auto insurance to start driving on the right side of the road with a vehicle where the wheel is on the left. I will be forever grateful to all those who helped one way or another during this season in my life.

Within a week or so, I went to my nearest neighbors' houses and introduced myself to them because I felt that it was essential to do so as a newcomer in a neighborhood. One of the neighbor's family name was Newhouse. Upon returning to my studio, I thought they said that their house was new, which was kind of ironic considering the fact that house was in a historic district, and it looked old. Later, it was confirmed that their family name was in fact Newhouse and not the house that was new.

I believe it is valuable for newcomers to introduce themselves to their closest neighbors as well as their local government and community leaders when they move into an unfamiliar area. As customary, I made several attempts to schedule a visit with the Wake Forest mayor, Vivian A. Jones, but was not successful due my school schedule and the mayor's availability.

Anyway, it did not take me long to realize that the heat in North Carolina has humidity, which was the opposite of Haiti and Jamaica (and probably for the rest of the Caribbean countries where summer is usually hot, but dry). During the summertime in the Caribbean, people typically sit in their backyard to enjoy a cool breeze, but that was not so for North Carolina.

I used some part of the summer to reflect and ponder on my life and try to make sense of what God was trying to teach me about life. I began to feel the need to go deeper into the water of ministry through ordination and started to feel more comfortable with being a minister.

My dad used to tell me not to be engaged in anything without talking to God first, asking Him for guidance and wisdom. I prayed and fasted about the ordination idea. The more I prayed, the more I realized that this was the right course of action to take especially if I planned to be in ministry full time.

Some mentors I spoke with told me that being ordained is a solemn ministerial commitment; therefore, it should not be taken lightly. They encouraged me to think seriously about it and ask God for wisdom.

Weeks later, it was time to start the 2006 fall semester. I made an appointment to meet with one of my ministerial professors at the divinity school. I shared with him how I had been thinking about ordination. He suggested I complete my first year of divinity school, then pursue ordination. He also reminded me that ordination is a commitment to God and His people through service.

Ordination and Challenges

In the Spring of 2007, I officially started my second year in the divinity program. My ordination was scheduled for Sunday, April 29, 2007. To prepare, I met with my church board and then with an ordination committee to answer questions. One of my assignments was to imagine I was in an elevator going to the next floor with someone who asked me to explain my understanding of God, Jesus Christ, and the Holy Spirit.

At the end, one committee member asked me if I intended to have a family. At first, I wondered aloud, "What does that question have to do with ordination? That is my personal business!" Before I could answer, he challenged me to think and ponder about that

112

question because ministry would not be able to help me provide a better life for them. I left that meeting furious but in retrospect I thanked God for that challenge.

I will never forget my ordination experience. It was over-whelming to see family from Haiti and Florida, my godmother from Indianapolis, Indiana, a lady I was dating and loved ones from Connecticut, and relatives, colleagues, congregants, and new friends I had made in Wake Forest, NC.

My godmother and I after my ordination service

Some families, relatives, friends, and my godmother who
attended my ordination!

My Pastor, Rev. Dick Graves, sharing something with me!

My late preaching professor, Dr. Roy DeBrand, and his wife also
delivered the homily!

To my surprise, even a local newspaper, *The Wake Weekly*, Wake Forest, NC, was in attendance to cover the ceremony. An article, *Haitian Sensation*, was published a week later.

To me, an ordination is the most important service or day in a minister's life. I was astonished to see how my divinity school family came to support me and celebrate with me. Looking back, I have come to realize that people we meet on our journey enlarge our family, whereas our family of origin seems to decrease.

About one week after being ordained as a clergy, I was finally able to meet with the mayor of Wake Forest, Vivian A. Jones. Upon entering her office, I was received enthusiastically, and as I was about to introduce myself, she interrupted me and said, "I know who you are. I read an article about you in the Wake Weekly newspaper." She then welcomed me to the Wake Forest community. We chatted for about thirty minutes, and while I was leaving, she wished me the best on my graduate studies. I will forever cherish that experience simply because of her warmth as well as her meekness as a politician.

My professors challenged me academically and spiritually. They always challenged me to aim for ministerial excellency while ministering to God's people.

Sometimes I was confused by traditions versus what the Bible really taught. I came to comprehend that learning takes place in the confusion or gray moments as opposed to the "black-and-white periods." We are in great danger the moment we think we fully understand everything.

The Unanswered Question and Wedding Fever

When I was 18 years old, I wrote a 16-year-old young lady a letter asking if I could date her. I knew she received that letter because the mail carrier was one of my older sisters. Still, I never heard back. About two years later, she migrated to the U.S and five years later I went to Jamaica to study. Through a family friend, we were able to reconnect at the end of summer 2006. I asked her if she had received the letter I sent, and she told me she still had it. We began dating long-distance. My ego was still bruised because of her silent rejection.

I used any opportunity to travel to her state even just for a weekend. Her parents approved of our relationship and things were going well, so far. One of the things I used to do while dating was to ask hypothetical questions with the goal to feel the temperature of that emotional relationship and its future.

For instance, while on a casual date with that lady in her hometown, I invited her to visit jewelry stores so that I would know the type of ring she liked if and when I wanted to take our courtship to a higher level. While in a mall, she looked at different rings and tried them. Then, she told me that she would like a ring that cost between $5,000.00 to $10,000.00 because she understood the fact that I was a fulltime student.

She went on to say if I were working, however, she would have wanted a more expensive one because she would not want her friends to see her wearing a cheap ring with a small diamond. I could not believe what I was hearing, but I did my best to hide my emotions. I was speechless to say the least. After gathering my thoughts, I told her that wearing an expensive wedding ring with a big diamond would not guarantee a successful marriage, and she told me that she did not care.

During the course of that courtship, she made it clear that she did not want to marry a clergy person. This was a major concern to me because I had made up my mind to be in ministry for the rest of my life. Weeks before my ordination ceremony, I told her as she and her family planned to come to NC that I would appreciate if she could keep her hair natural instead of wearing a wig and she agreed. To my dismay, she wore one with two distinct colors on it. I was not pleased to say the least. My disappointment was obvious because her oldest sister inquired about my cold demeanor upon seeing her less than forty-eight hours before the ceremony.

Throughout the relationship, there were red flags but the ring one, to keep up with her friends, was the last straw that broke the camel's back. Subsequently, I began slowly planning my exit because I realized that she was not the person I thought I could spend the rest of my life with.

Also, if I were to continue, it would be a lifetime of competition amongst her and her friends. The bottom line was that relationship would have been too taxing. Hence, keeping up with the Joneses tends to leave people in debt or broke.

By summer 2007, she began sending some hints about how some of her friends were getting married and she was excited for them. She was even a maid of honor in one or two weddings. I ignored those hints and finally told her that I was not ready to be engaged. I wanted to complete my graduate studies; it was my main priority. Her attitude toward me changed completely.

To make a long story short, after praying, thinking, and pondering over the whole situation, I informed her that it would be better for us to quit dating because of our fundamental disagreements. Subsequently, I was shocked, insulted, and emotionally hurt by her nasty attitude and statement when she told me that I would have begged her to marry her if she were a US citizen and had money. I made myself unequivocally clear to her that I would not be forced into marrying. Based on her strange attitude, she gave me the impression that she was experiencing wedding fever as many of her friends were being married. I thought she was the love of my life, but I was wrong.

As her family knew of our relationship, I informed her father of my decision as her mother was not available to talk at that time. Her dad already knew about the breakup from his daughter. Then, he asked me why. I told him that his daughter and I had major irreconcilable differences but one of the main ones had to do with the fact that she did not want to be in a long-term relationship with a man of the cloth. Suddenly, he rhetorically asked, "Would she rather marry a *Ougan,* that is a male priest in the Haitian vodou religion?" His wife, on the other hand, declined to talk to me for now according to her husband and promised to call me back.

Weeks later, her mother called and apologized for refusing to talk to me when I spoke with her husband because she did not want to say anything to me at that time and regreted it later. She continued by saying that she could have given me a piece of her mind that day because she was mad, but out of respect she decided not to talk. I thanked her for exercising self-control.

At the end of our conversation, she suggested that I date a caucasian lady from the local church where I was a minister so that I would not have to leave America upon completing my master's degree. I thanked her for thinking about my future and told her that I never thought of that possibility, which I felt was an odd advice.

Despite ending that relationship, I tried to be civil with that family by wishing them Merry Christmas and Happy New Year either by mailing a Christmas card or by calling them. One year, I called her oldest sister (with whom I had a healthy relationship) and after introducing myself, she told me that she knew who I was and warned me not to ever call her family again and she hung up. Based on her out of character reaction, I concluded that she was still furious with me for breaking up with her sister.

Anyway, after taking a couple of counseling courses, I discovered that I might have a passion for Clinical Pastoral Education (CPE). I completed my first level of CPE at a WakeMed Health and Hospitals in Raleigh and in Zebulon as an intern in the summer of 2008.

At the end of my internship experience, as I reflected on my experiences since high school, I noticed a pattern of chaplaincy involvement from Cap-Haitien, Haiti, to Kingston, Jamaica.

I appreciate self-examination because it helps in reviewing one's achievements and shortcomings. Human beings should have both because no one is perfect. After examining my life in context, I felt the urge to go deeper into chaplaincy. I applied at the same local hospital in their residency program and was accepted to start on Wednesday, September 1, 2010.

Due to my interest in world religions, especially Islam and Jehovah's Witnesses, I spent one year as an intern at the World Religions and Global Cultures Center (WRGCC) at that same university under the leadership of a distinguished professor, George Braswell.

There are many things that happened during my divinity school journey; however, for the sake of time I will only share two of them. I was honored and blessed when my parents asked my oldest brother who is also a minister and me to perform their fifty-fifth wedding anniversary ceremony.

My mom told me that he wanted me to be the one to deliver the homily and bless the new rings as I was the youngest. What an honor! The ceremony was breathtaking. The best part was when I said to my dad, "You may kiss your wife." The sanctuary was filled with laughter.

The second event was a sad one. On Friday, November 28, 2008, the day after Thanksgiving, one of my brothers told me that our dad passed away. Days later, I began making preparation to travel back home to be with my mom and the rest of the family.

It was difficult and an emotionally challenging moment to preach at my dad's funeral, but I felt compelled to do it because who I was becoming was a result of God and my parents. I thank God for the exemplary life my dad lived. Through those years I had known him, I must say that he lived what he preached. He was my hero.

The divinity school was incredibly supportive during my grieving journey. Arrangements were made to reschedule my final exams for the 2008 fall semester. I felt like they understood my emotional state of mind, and I was not alone though I was grieving. It is amazing how a little gesture can make a world of difference in one's life during a difficult and challenging time.

I was able to take some summer classes because I was determined to complete the program in four years with my specializations in homiletics, biblical languages, and chaplaincy. It was hard and discouraging at times, but I thank God that I never gave up, although I considered quitting many times.

Sugar Mama's Offer

During my graduate studies, I was introduced to a lady through a mutual friend. She was nice, easy to talk to, and could carry a good intellectual conversation. We could talk about any topic and had respectful debates. She was well versed in current affairs.

Gradually, our friendship had grown into something else and from the outset, I informed her that I did not think that our courtship would have a future because of our age difference. She told me that we would not know unless we tried. About a month later, she informed me that she could assist me in changing my immigration status from an international student into a permanent resident card holder in about six months as she was a US citizen.

Consequently, as I pondered to make sense of that offer, it became apparent that I would have to marry her in order for that to happen. I thanked her for thinking about my current status and told her I would share my decision with her. Frankly, I felt like things were going too fast especially with that offer. As a result, I even questioned my decision to be in that relationship in the first place.

Apparently, she noticed my cold feet about her immigration proposal and said to me that giving a permanent immigration status would not be the only thing she could offer me. She said that once we were married, she would add my name in her health insurance policy with the company she worked for and I would have access to topnotch healthcare services, including dental and vision.

With all those offers on the table, I was confused and tempted to give it a try. Generally, I do not talk much during my confusion. As a result, I told her that I would need to process everything and would share my decision with her. She probably sensed my reluctance, and suddenly added that once we married she would add my name on her life insurance policy as the sole beneficiary.

I must admit that she was generous throughout our relationship. She was always ready to assist me financially. As an international student that was tempting because I was in need and yet, for some reason, did not feel too comfortable accepting her gifts all the time. Candidly, deep in my heart I felt like I was being trapped and moreover, things were going too fast and with too many promises. Numerous times, she urged me to inform her of my needs and she would take me shopping. I felt like it was too good to be true!

One day, my car broke down and my mechanic informed me that it would need a new transmission, which would cost roughly $3,000.00. Thankfully, I was able to use a car from a friend for as long as I needed during my school commute. I chose not to mention my car problem to her because knowing her she would want to help. To this day, I still do not know how she knew about my car issue even though I was not forthcoming with her when she realized that I was driving another vehicle.

One day while driving around, she took me to a car dealership to choose a vehicle. I reminded her that as an international student I would not be able to afford to buy one. She told me that not to worry about it, for now, that I could reimburse her when I started working. For some reason, I still did not feel at ease with that payment arrangement, and we left the dealership. About a week later, she told me that one of her colleagues was about to buy a newer vehicle and was selling the other one for about $2,000.00 and she wanted to buy it for me as a Christmas gift to which I declined because again I felt like it was still too good to be true.

Less than a month later, someone who had a black sport Honda Civic, sitting in his garage for a while, donated it to me. That was a blessing! After making some minor repairs, it was ready to be back on the road. I never had any major mechanical issues with it for the remainder of my almost two-and-half hour commute twice a week in two years.

One of my sisters knew about my situation with that lady. When I shared my predicament with her, she told me that there was no age when it came to love and advised me to proceed. Then, I told her that it was highly possible that my fatherhood dream would be dead and that was my biggest concern. "Do not worry,

122

my brother! You have plenty of nephews and nieces that you could consider them and treat them as your children." She stated. I was shocked and disappointed by her statement and said nothing to her. I tend to become speechless whenever I am stunned while thinking or pondering an unusual situation.

Several months into the relationship, after much thinking and pondering over everything, I concluded that it was not going to work out especially with the age gap between us. She was about fifteen years older than me. Consequently, the possibility of having children would be challenging, medically. Therefore, my biggest dream to become a biological father would be in limbo with her age situation.

I finally had the courage to tell her that I did not think there was a future between us. She was devastated and angry, to say the least. She accused me of not knowing what I wanted in life. She also reminded me that she was ready and willing to transform my life for the better, saying I was stupid for rejecting her and her proposals. I peacefully listened.

After she finished expressing her emotions, I reminded her how nice and generous she had been to me during those months and how I appreciated her desires to make my life better. Then, she said that she respected my honesty, but never wanted to talk to me again.

While examining the whole situation, I must admit that she was a kind-hearted and generous lady. However, I had to look beyond her generosity and her offers, which were pretty tempting. If she were my age, the relationship could have survived because she was both beautiful inside and out.

Chapter Nine

Death, Love, and Earthquake

As I mentioned in the previous chapter, I faced two challenges. The second one had to do with finding love after the funeral of my biological father, which I never thought possible (considering the emotional circumstance).

Burying my Daddy

When I went back home to burry my dad, I never thought my emotional life would be affected as well. My dad was buried on Saturday, December 6, 2008. Culturally speaking, the following days and, sometimes, weeks would be for visitation; relatives and family friends would come to continue providing comfort and support to the grieving family.

The next day after taking an early cat nap, I went to the living room to greet some of those people who came to support us, as is customary to do. This is a great custom because grief can be a long journey and very painful, emotionally. Having support tends to ease the pain a little. Unfortunately, many industrialized countries, especially the capitalist ones have a propensity to rush a grieved person into going back to work as soon as possible because time is money. I tend to call it a microwave grief. Sooner or later, many of those countries will experience the aftermath in a negative way because an unresolved grieved person is a dangerous one, which could lead to complicated actions.

Tactlessly, many people tend to put a time limit on a grieving person. It is a journey and not a destination, and it varies from person to person. There seems to be a one-size-fits all mindset about grief. Bear in mind, each individual comes with his or her own size! Grief can become complicated if not dealt with properly and professionally, leading to mental issues.

As I was saying, many people came to grieve with my family. After thanking everyone for coming and telling them how much it meant to my family, one of my sisters, Violette, introduced me to one of her friends, Nelcie Voltaire. We chatted for several minutes and then she was about to leave. Before she left, I thanked her individually for coming to pay a visit. As she was leaving, Violette asked if I could use her car to take her friend home as she did not drive. The distance from my sister's home to her friend's was less than five miles and I was silent all the way to the final destination. I thanked her once again and I went back to my sister's home.

Upon arriving, I heard someone crying and I jokingly said, "Who else died?" I was told that my twin nephews were horseplaying and one of their heads hit a concrete wall and blood was everywhere. A towel had to be used to put pressure on the cut as it was deep before going to the Emergency Department.

In Haiti, who you know and how much money you have tend to determine how long one will be in any ED. Unfortunately, those things tend to be the determining factors in terms of the kind of medical service one will receive. Immediately, Violette called her friend (the one I had just taken home) as she is a pediatrician, by profession, and she agreed to go the ED with us. Voilà! In less than two hours, we were heading back home. They had to stitch that laceration and had given us a pain killer to be used later, as needed.

Once everything was over, I chauffeured Dr. Voltaire to her home. I thanked her for her willingness to assist with that unexpected ordeal. "Never mind! It was my pleasure to assist." She replied. I told her that accompanying us to the hospital meant a lot to me and I knew that I would never be able to repay her. Nevertheless, I asked to take her out for ice cream.

The first ice cream social date went well. Before I returned to the United States of America, we went out for ice cream twice. As a result, a relationship was born. The day before I left my hometown to travel back to the USA, she asked me for my overseas phone number to check on me once I arrived. Honestly, I gave it to her and was not expecting a phone call upon arrival, but I was wrong. While I was with one of my brothers heading to his home, she called to check if I had made it safely. I was impressed by that gesture, it showed that she cared.

Finding Love... Will You Marry Me?

Weeks later, we graduated to friendship from a relationship. We remained friends for a couple of months and on my birthday, April 4, 2009, I asked her if she wanted to take our friendship to a deeper emotional level. During that time, she would come to the USA for medical continuing education. I always made sure I drove to that location to see her.

Through this experience and others, distance seemed minute because of love. For instance, I drove to Washington DC right after completing a long day at a local hospital during my chaplaincy internship because she was there for another medical training. I was in a traffic jam during rush hour in Virginia and we were on the phone chatting until I made it to my final destination.

During my long-distance courtship with Nelcie, we had the opportunity to go on an emotional date several times. Some great qualities were discovered. I began to see her as someone I could spend the rest of my life with, eventually. Case in point, she was brilliant and yet down to earth and simple. She was not extravagant or flashy but modest. In other words, she exhibited some qualities I thought were important in a potential life partner.

Eight months later, I started planning my next emotional move to be more serious by proposing to her. But being in a long-distance relationship was challenging in terms of creativity even though I intended to pop that question face-to-face when I went to my hometown, Cap-Haitien, during the Christmas break.

Nevertheless, before I asked her the big question, while she was in America for a medical continuing education training, I invited her to a mall to look at engagement rings if and when I would like to propose to her. I showed her a ring with a large size diamond on it. With a surprise look on her face, she asked me if I was serious about the size of that diamond to which I asked her what she thought.

Subsequently, she said, "If and when you were going to propose to me, I would like you to know that I would love the smallest diamond on that ring because I do not like flashy jewelry." When I insisted, she calmly said, "If you were to buy something like that, I would return it and exchange it for something modest because wearing a big diamond means nothing to me." That experience supported my observation of her as someone who could become my life partner because of her simplicity.

In the meantime, I wanted to start giving her some clues about my plan. I began sending her an email while in the USA about fourteen days before Friday, December 25, 2009, to ask "Will you marry me?" as that question has fourteen letters. Beginning with the first email, I made sure I used a word that started with a *W*, I increased the font size (to make it stand out), bolded it, and italicized it. I did the same for each letter throughout all those emails each day until the morning of that big day before we departed to a local beach with some of our inner circle friends.

We dated for eight months through an international, long-distance relationship. On Friday, December 25, 2009, we went to the beach in our hometown with some friends who were co-conspirators, and I asked her to marry me. She was shocked and speechless, to say the least. I was on my one of my knees for less than thirty seconds, but it felt like thirty minutes before she said yes.

Days later, we talked about those hints from those fourteen emails, and I revealed my intention. Then, she told me that it was kind of weird reading those emails daily with one word standing out from the other ones.

Challenging a Tradition

I had broken away from the engagement tradition of the Haitian culture because I never liked the way it was done. Conventionally, both boyfriend and girlfriend are present as well as their parents. In most cases, however, the gentleman had to plan everything behind the prospective fiancée's back, in secret arrangement with both sets of parents.

For instance, this is usually done over a dinner party. After asking for everyone's attention, he would inquire the parents of the lady their blessing and then pop up the question to the lady, "Will you marry me?" Once she responds affirmatively, the party becomes an engagement ceremony.

I think an emotional engagement should be as intimate as possible with one or two closest friends present to take pictures or videotape that emotional and precious moment. In my case, for instance, I had informed my mom and my siblings about my plan but told them it was not going to be done the traditional way. Of course, some were not pleased about it because they were so used to the way it had been done for decades, but I told them it was my decision to make.

I, however, believe that the newly engaged couple should formally announce their engagement to their parents and loved ones afterward. Coincidentally, Nelcie thought the same way about the tradition.

Many Haitian parents like being involved in their children's emotional business. Hence, some in-laws tend to create drama. Their intentions, at times, are just for the sake of gossiping;

especially if they did not approve the relationship in the first place. However, they would pretend to show concern. I have witnessed this firsthand within my family of origin as well in my professional life as a pastoral counselor. In-laws can make or break a young family if married couples permit them. The newlyweds have to be strong and supportive of each of other and proactive in setting boundaries.

When there are no walls around an emotional relationship, especially in a marriage, anybody can come in and distort things. Be mindful that setting frontiers may make some unhappy people. As a result, they may say things like "so and so has changed" or "that spouse has caused our son or daughter not to love us anymore." Inviting family members into one's relationship or marriage may lead to potential chaos because their emotions are involved; therefore, it is highly possible their judgement would be clouded. Strangely enough, a complete stranger might be in better position to share some sound guidance.

Friday, December 25, 2009, was one of the memorable days of my life because it was the day I asked Nelcie to marry me. Days later, I introduced her, as my fiancée, to my mother and siblings. Everything went well for the most part. One of my sisters, on the other hand, was tenacious about knowing our wedding date. We told her that we would inform everybody when we were ready. By the look on her face, I could tell she was not satisfied with that answer.

Independence Day and Pumpkin Soup

We went to church on New Year's Eve as it is a tradition to be in a worship service at the end of a year. That religious worship service usually ended after midnight, and as soon as everything was over, people started wishing each other Happy New Year and Happy Independence Day.

Haiti was a French colony. During the enslavement of people who were brought from the continent of Africa, against their will, to labor on plantations all over in North America. At that time, Haiti was one of the wealthiest of those colonies. It was nicknamed the pearl of the Caribbean. Its main productions were coffee and sugar.

Those slaves' labors varied from working in the fields to performing house chores for their masters and one of them was cooking. The sad part was those slaves were not allowed to eat the meals that they had cooked. The ones for those masters were more nutritious, and those cooked for them were not. Pumpkin soup was one of most prestigious and delicious meals, and again, slaves were not allowed to partake from it even though they were the chefs.

In 1791, the enslaved Haitians said enough was enough and began revolting against the status quo. After a decade of strategizing and fighting the most powerful army in the world, the Napoleon Army, the decisive battle led by Jean Jacques Dessalines was held on November 18, 1803, in Vertières, Cap-Haitian. In 1804, they took their independence from France, and Haiti became the first black republic in the world.

It was and still is one of the biggest defeats France has ever faced. To put that loss into the twentieth century context, imagine the most powerful army in the world being defeated by an island or developing country.

Freedom cannot be given; it has to be taken by force because the oppressor would never let go of their power. Being powerful is one of the most dangerous positions to be in because those in power tend to think only of themselves. The powerless, after a while, will be empowered by their condition to challenge the status quo, which will eventually lead to a family, local, statewide, nationwide, and worldwide revolt.

On January 1, 1803, the freed slaves sent a message to France by cooking pumpkin soup and drinking it, to let their oppressors know they were free just like them. From then on, drinking pumpkin soup on Independence Day became a national tradition.

Earthquake in the Midst of Love

After formally introducing my fiancée to my family, it was my turn to take my mom to meet Nelcie's mom and make it official. A date and time were set for my mom and I to go to Nelcie's home. On that day, while I was waiting for my mom to be ready, I felt our house trembling at about 5:50 PM for several seconds. At first, I thought it was a trailer driving nearby that has caused the jolting. Minutes later, we were on our way to check a box off on the cultural to-do-list.

Upon arriving, I re-introduced my mom to Nelcie's mom and informed them of our engagement. While talking, someone came and suggested we turn on our television because there had been a massive earthquake, magnitude 7.0, and its epicenter was in the capital, Port-au-Prince on Tuesday, January 12, 2010.

That was the end of the official engagement reunion. We were speechless, in disbelief, and became frozen. Right there, everyone began calling their loved ones living in Port-au-Prince to check on them. Haiti's communication system was down.

As a result, frustration and anxiety started to mount. We did not know what to do. We felt powerless and helpless. I encouraged everyone to pray for peace and comfort while waiting for the communication system to return to normal so that we could check on relatives. Consequently, we concluded the formal introductory fellowship and left.

That day will be forever engraved in my memory, witnessing the devastation of some parts of my country on live television. I had heard many survivor stories. People of all ages died. Some were buried alive, others spent days under rubble. According to several news reports, one person was rescued after twenty-seven days. Some people's lives were changed forever because of that natural disaster. "Between four-to-six thousand people had become physically disabled."[14] In addition to the physical distress, the mental impact was at a national level. All Haitians, one way or another, were negatively affected by the earthquake.

I was caught between two worlds. I wanted to stay to help my fellow Haitians but, on the other hand, I was scheduled to start my last semester in the divinity school program on Tuesday, January 19, 2010. After processing the whole situation, I decided that the best thing to do, at that moment, was to go back to America to complete my graduate studies. My fiancée was scheduled to resume work in two weeks but was called to go back to work as soon as possible because medical helicopters were bringing survivors to a Catholic hospital, Sacred Heart, where she worked as a pediatrician and head of the pediatric department.

In the meantime, friends in Jamaica, the United States, and other places kept calling and emailing me to check if my family and I were okay. The outpouring of support was excellent. There was a spirit of concern. All international flights departing from Haiti were cancelled.

As a result, my divinity school family started a process to make necessary arrangements with an airline to fly me to the USA. Since the day I entered the divinity school until my last day, I always felt special. It was a great feeling when professors saw you on campus and greeted you by your name.

There was and still is a powerful sense of family community, at Campbell, with genuine love at its center. Through a local ministerial connection, I was able to travel to the neighboring country, Dominican Republic, and then fly to America. Upon arriving at RDU, almost the whole congregation from my local church came to welcome me. At first, they thought I was dead after being

---

[14] https://bit.ly/3yQDpMt - Access date: 8.15.2021

engaged. They had expressed their joy to see me back safe and sound. I told them how scared I was during some aftershocks.

As I stated earlier, my fiancée and I celebrated our first Independence Day together and drank some pumpkin soup. On that day, after debating different dates we concluded to have our religious wedding ceremony on Saturday, May 15, 2010, the day after my graduation to kill two birds with one stone.

Weeks prior to our big day, we applied for a marriage license, and days later we had a private ceremony (see picture below) at one of our dearest friends, Delores Pruitt (next to Nelcie on her left), who has been like a mother to us. Since arriving in NC, she has been instrumental in my life and later in my family's.

Left to right: Rev. Dick Graves, Edisson (me), my fiancée (Nelcie), Ms. Delores, Mrs. Susan Moss (a retired church pianist), and Mrs. Ginger Graves

Carpooling Leads to Friendship

I spent four years driving about three hours round trip twice a week. One week after starting the master's program, I found out about that another student, André Turrentine, lived about thirty minutes from my host family. He agreed to give me a ride to school

134

as long as someone dropped me off at his home and picked me up in the evening. In the meantime, the process of having a car to drive was being worked out.

Meanwhile, several congregants agreed to take me to my colleague's home and others picked me up upon returning from school. Weeks later, after receiving my driving license, André and I began carpooling and it was a relief for both of us as we had alternated the driving role. It was also a respite for my volunteer chauffeurs from my local church. I will be forever grateful for their ministry toward my graduate schooling.

It did not take long to feel like I was part of André's family. One day, I started feeling a sore throat and some discomfort on our way back from school. As soon as he noticed that he called his wife, Karlene (who is a practicing attorney) and asked if she could prepare some tea and soup for me. At the end, they urged me to stay with them as they were concerned for me being in a studio by myself. It was ministry in action.

Spending time with people can, indeed, create friendship, fellowship, and eventually develop a certain level of trust. Consequently, André and I became exceptionally good friends. I also developed healthy relationship with his family. He had also become my confidante when I was thinking about taking my friendship with Nelcie to an emotional level. As a matter of fact, he was present when I asked Nelcie on the phone if she was willing to be on an emotional journey with me.

About three years into the divinity school program, we could no longer continue to carpool due to different classes' schedules. Not being able to commute together anymore did not stop our friendship. We remained friends and continued fellowshipping whenever we could, even though we were busy. Throughout those four years, we never got in a car accident. We had, however, seen many crashes. Looking back, God was good to us during our long commute! Rev. André Turrentine is the founder and pastor of Shepherds in The Field ministry, Raleigh, NC.

Driving Over the Speeding Limit...Or Driving While Black

I had begun driving regularly when I migrated to Jamaica in my early twenties to study. It was then I had first seen people driving on the left side of the road and the steering wheel of a vehicle was on the right. It was a cultural shock and I quickly made up my mind that I would never try to drive in Jamaica. I was terrified and frozen whenever I thought about resuming my driving skill.

As a passenger, I always felt like vehicles coming toward the car would crash into us. Slowly and surely, I started to feel comfortable with the new traffic system. After migrating to Kingston to attend Jamaica Theological Seminary, I decided it was time to face my traffic anxiety. Subsequently, I found myself driving with the assistance of a friend.

After examining that experience and other ones, being afraid of anything can make or break someone if not dealt with appropriately. I was and still am grateful to that person who challenged me to do something I, first, thought was impossible. Within weeks, I found myself driving like all the other drivers. As a matter of fact, I had forgotten my traffic phobia.

During those four years of driving twice a week for classes, a highway patrol officer once stopped me. He asked me for my driving license and proof of insurance. I was nervous, shocked, and began sweating. I gave him all the requested documents, so I thought. "Sir, did you realize what you just gave me?" The officer asked. It was then I noticed that I had given him my debit card instead of my driving license. I promptly apologized and confessed that it was the first time I was stopped in my driving experience.

He seemed to understand my faux pas; nevertheless, gave me a ticket anyway for going three miles over the speed limit, which was later dismissed by a traffic judge based on my safe driving record. Looking back, that officer could have interpreted the giving of my bank card instead of my driving license action as bribery and used it as an excuse to arrest me. I was glad it was only a traffic violation.

Defending my Dissertation and Graduating

There was no better way to end my academic chapter than to begin a brand new one the next day with somebody I plan to spend the rest of my life with. If someone were to tell me that I would have met my wife-to-be after burying my father, I would say no way. Nevertheless, I was ready to commence this new emotional phase in life with my fiancée the day after my graduation.

Before I knew it, I was a senior in the Master of Divinity program. I had two new major challenges to face. My research dissertation paper was due in April 2010. Once the research was completed, I had to meet with several professors and defend my thesis.

With my dissertation director, Dr. Bruce Powers,
after submitting and defending my thesis!

137

There was a feeling of accomplishment after presenting and defending my dissertation. I received some positive feedback and some constructive critique. There is one word all researchers hope to hear at the end, "Congratulations!" I was thrilled to hear that word.

My academic advisor suggested I consider a joint program with an MDiv and Juris Doctor degree because he thought I would be good at it, but I declined, intending to stick with only theology.

On the last chapel service at the divinity school, I was asked to share a few words about my theological experience during those four years. At the end of my speech, I told the audience that after completing four years studying theology in relationship with God and humanity, I concluded that I still have a long way to go in my quest. That pursuit, my friends, is an endless one.

Weeks later came the day I had been waiting for, graduation. There was a feeling of "mission accomplished." People traveled from Haiti, Jamaica, Canada, different towns in south Florida, Alabama, New Jersey, New York, Maryland, and North Carolina to celebrate with me and my wife-to-be, in our wedding, the next day.

Receiving my master degree from the academic
dean, Dr. Michael G. Cogdill

Chapter Ten

Big Events...Graduation and Wedding

Throughout my journey, I have come to realize that God sometimes has a way of sending the right people into my life at the right place and time. One needs to be on alert, ready, and keep an open mind because surprises might come when they are least expected. God is always on time. His timing is perfect.

It is my responsibility, with God's help, to be prepared and ready to use my gifts, skills, and talents when opportunities come. I also believe that, sometimes, we may have to create those opportunities in order to meet people's needs if we could see them before they arise. Therefore, proactive ministry should be one of the most effective methods of the twentieth century and beyond.

Saturday, May 15, 2010, the big day! I was excited and yet nervous. I have always considered marriage to be one of the biggest emotional commitments a person could ever make. To make a love that was private, public, and to cherish and appreciate that individual in good and in challenging times. To love that person with the hope of understanding her or him in all seasons.

The maid of honor was one of my wife's friends. For the best man, it was my brother, Joshua. Years prior, I was his best man at his wedding ceremony. We made that promise while practicing martial arts in Haiti. Promises made, promises kept!

My best man

The ceremony was simple, short, and sweet. My former room-mate, Charlie, of three months when I stayed with my US host family and my goddaughter, Loudjina, from New Jersey, read some verses from the Christian sacred text.

My goddaughter and former roommate

On a side note, my goddaughter is a proactive planner. Weeks after I shared my engagement plan with her, she mailed me a letter requesting to be my firstborn's godmother if and when my wife and I had children. Less than two years later, she became the godmother of our first son, Matthis. As I am writing this memoir, she is in the process of completing her Bachelor of Science in Nursing.

All eyes are on the bride!

Ready to tie the knot!

It's official!

My biological mom

Our Jamaican sister, Charene, singing, and
our mom, Phyllis, signing

Families of origin with in-laws, nieces, and nephews

Relatives and Family Friends

Sharing a hug with my Jamaican mom, Phyllis

Our American family

On a side note, that lady and her husband were ones of the collaborators in secretly planning the private engagement party. She is also a trained pediatrician. Four years later, she and her husband, Dr. Bertrand Saintilnord, MD, became the godparents of our second son, Edwards.

My wife's colleague, Dr. Mikaelle Baltazard Saintilnor, MD

Friends from High School, College Pratique du Nord, Cap-Haitien, Haiti, and Northern Caribbean University, Mandeville, Jamaica

Once the religious ceremony was over, I was shocked and surprised to see some faculty members as well as friends from Campbell University Divinity School who had come to celebrate with us on our memorable day.

Some of my Campbell University Divinity School Families

My US family as well as my church families worked tirelessly to plan all the details and to make sure that everything went as planned. Honestly, it would have been almost impossible for Nelcie and I to plan our wedding while she was in Haiti working and I was in the US completing my final semester as a graduate student.

With the help of technology, however, she was able to give her blessings on almost everything and also made some suggestions. My wife and I are forever grateful to our loved ones, friends, colleagues, our Jamaican and US adoptive parents, and church families for their support on our wedding day. It was a success!

My godmother had been present in many major events in my life. On that special occasion, however, she could not make it because she was in an assisted living facility in Indianapolis, IN. Her presence and personality were greatly missed.

Our post wedding plan before the January 12, 2010, earthquake that hit our country, Haiti, was for me to go back home to find employment at a local seminary and eventually start a new job on the other side of the state. In the meantime, my wife would continue working as a pediatrician.

As a result, we had to reconsider our original plan because the damage was enormous; planning to start and raise a young family there would be a challenge because of the lack of basic medical material. We concluded that I would start my chaplaincy residency, she would come every three to six months, and we would ultimately make a final decision upon completing my residency. Hopefully, things would start improving back home for us to return for good, to start our family.

As we were planning our first Christmas, my wife suggested that we travel to Indianapolis to spend that special day with our godmother in her facility as she could not make it to our wedding. I was speechless and honored by Nelcie's recommendation to visit and meet her godmother-in-law during that family season.

Two smart and wise ladies

It was a sacred moment for us to be with her at her last stop in a nursing home. All of us have a final stop to make before our final destination and it may vary from person to person. Our pilgrimage on earth may include many exits, but all trips will end one way or another.

I was and still am grateful to my wife for agreeing to travel all the way to Indianapolis from North Carolina especially in the middle of winter. Mentally, my godmother was sharp. She recounted many stories of me growing up from her countless trips to Haiti and was able to share them with my wife.

About two years later, I went back to Indianapolis, IN, to celebrate my godmother's life through a homegoing service. I was honored and humbled to deliver the eulogy. She dedicated her life to impact people's lives positively for God's glory. She had many children, grandchildren, and great grandchildren without ever giving birth biologically. She was an exceptionally caring human being with no visible hidden agenda who expected nothing in return.

Ready to share some comforting words at my godmother's
funeral service in Indianapolis, IN!

During our trip to and from Indianapolis, my wife kept telling me that she was having some unexplainable feelings. We had come up with several hypotheses of that strange sensation. One week after upon returning to North Carolina, we had found out that we were all wrong with our hypotheses because after some tests it was revealed that we were pregnant with our first child.

We were thrilled by that news. My wife and I had developed a proactive mentality early in our relationship. Being proactive does not mean that one is anxious. It is about hoping for the best while preparing for the worst-case scenarios. In other words, look at all potential aspects of a situation for possible outcomes and how we might eventually deal with it.

Five months into our marriage, for instance, we both went to see medical specialists to make sure that everything was in order, medically, when it came to the possibility of being pregnant. We were not being pessimistic or anxious. We went if in the event that there was a medical irregularity that needed some treatment, to correct it now rather than later.

Sometimes waiting for years before completing a medical checkup might be too late. I was ready and willing to do whatever it would take if I had some reproductive issues. Unfortunately, some men in our society tend to feel that they were born to impregnate a lady. That type of thinking might boost a male's ego, but one might be shocked to know the percentage of men who are infertile. "Infertility affects an estimated 15% of couples globally, amounting to 48.5 million couples. Males are found to be solely responsible for 20-30% of infertility cases and contribute to 50% of cases overall."[15]

---

[15] https://bit.ly/32xoQRF - Access date: 9.2.2021

Chapter Eleven

Honeymoon and the Jamaican drug, Cannabis

Before the wedding, my wife-to-be, Nelcie, and I were counting down to our big day. We were excited throughout the planning process. We wanted to make sure that everything went as planned, especially the religious worship service. The wedding ceremony was well attended by loved ones and relatives from various places around the world, friends and colleagues from Campbell University Divinity School, and of course my local church family.

When it comes to friendship, I tend to make friends for life that eventually become like family. My adoptive Jamaican mom, Phyllis, and her oldest daughter, Charene (who I met early 2001 while attending a Seventh-day Adventist University in Mandeville, Jamaica), traveled to North Carolina for our wedding. She and her oldest daughter performed at the ceremony.

As mentioned earlier, Nelcie concluded that we should go to Jamaica for our honeymoon as I had lived there for six years, and we could travel around to various places on the island. She did not want to stay in a hotel the whole time where the only option was to go to the nearest local beach.

During the honeymoon planning stage, I spoke with my adoptive Jamaican dad about renting a car during my honeymoon and the possibility to introduce my wife to him (as he would not be able to come to the wedding). He, then, suggested that I used his wife's car instead of renting one.

My Wife Becomes my Nurse

Right after our wedding ceremony and reception ended, I experienced a sudden and excruciating headache while in the air during our trip from Raleigh Durham Airport (RDU), North Carolina, to Miami International Airport (MIA). It felt like my head was splitting into two halves. One of the flight attendants reported the

151

incident to the flight captain and they were planning to make an emergency landing.

The pain was so agonizing, tears began running on my cheeks, involuntarily. Then, my wife asked that flight attendant for some water. She pulled my handkerchief from my back pant pocket, dampened it with water, and put it on my forehead. Voila! Within minutes, that headache gradually had disappeared. The flight made it to its final destination without making that emergency landing for me to seek medical assistance.

What happened? I do not know. Nevertheless, after examining the whole situation, my theory was that my brain was extremely busy working on many projects at once such as, my graduate research paper, final exams, my school graduation, our wedding and honeymoon planning via technological means; and in less than twenty-four hours my brain had to start adjusting to its normal speed too fast.

Anyway, that incident did not stop our honeymoon plan. We spent the night in a local hotel near the airport and boarded another aircraft the next day to Montego Bay, Jamaica, where we spent two days. Then, we rode a public bus to Mandeville to stay with our adoptive Jamaican dad for two days; we visited the deaf school and fellowshipped with some of the children.

Getting High on Soup

After receiving the car with all its paperwork (in the event we were stopped by police), our adventure had started. It took me a few minutes to become accustomed to the traffic again because it had been many years since I drove on the left side of the road with the wheel on the right side. The Jamaican driving system is similar to England and some other countries in Europe.

We went to the capital, Kingston, to spend three days. It was there, that we visited the church where my former ministerial colleague could not remember my name while introducing Nelcie and me during a worship service. Right after church that day, we were on our way to Ocho Rios to be with one of my Seventh-day Adventist colleagues and his young family. Technically, the last time we were together was when we were students at Northern Caribbean University in Mandeville.

After dinner, my colleague and I chatted about almost everything while the wives fellowshipped. The next day, we planned to go to a local beach, but it was overcast, and no one was allowed to go into the water. We walked around the beach and took some pictures and bought some souvenirs.

My wife and I chilling out at a local vendor!

Later, another couple joined us, and we decided to eat dinner at a local restaurant. Minutes after settling, we were introduced to Jamaican soup as an appetizer, and we all ordered it. It was very tasty with good Caribbean seasoning. As most of us were half-way in our bowl, some of us began feeling dizzy, and within minutes the rest of us started experiencing some symptoms like dry mouth, distorted perception, relaxed state, sleepiness, feeling "high" or exhilaration. We stopped eating and called the waiter to inquire about the soup ingredients. To our bewilderment, some cannabis leaves were among the components.

We shared our grievance and dissatisfaction. After listening to their explanation, it was concluded that was a customary practice in restaurants to add some cannabis leaves in soup to enhance its flavor. We were also told that many people make tea with it as natural medicine. It has been reported that some local religious leaders would drink it before delivering their long sermons for stamina. Later, we all had a good laugh about that experience on our way home.

I was skeptical about those justifications because some people tend to find ways to justify their actions. It turned out I was wrong with my cynicism about that person's account. According to several sources on the internet as well as the most recent one from the Jamaica Gleaner, that is, the most respected local newspaper, "Cannabis is becoming part of the Jamaican cuisine."[16]

As they say, never say never in life when it comes to certain things. I never thought I would taste ganja in my life, nevertheless, experience its side effects. Due to being a second-hand ganja smoker while studying at that university or on the street, I never

---

[16] https://bit.ly/3ek76Mq - Access date: 9.10.2021

felt drugged by it. Over time, I could tell the difference between the smoke of a cigarette or cannabis.

I had lived in Jamaica for six years and had never shown any interest in trying it even though some people had encouraged me to do so countless times. For some reasons, I never had a desire whatsoever to attempt its use.

Chapter Twelve

Chaplaincy Internship and Residency Training

I was first exposed to the chaplaincy field while in high school at College Pratique du Nord (CPN), a Baptist institution in Cap-Haitian, Haiti, where there was a chaplain on staff. Once, I was asked to fill in as a chaplain student for three weeks in 1995, and later became the assistant chaplain for my remaining two years.

After having a dream about going into ministry, I migrated to Kingston, Jamaica, for formal ministerial training at Jamaica Theological Seminary (JTS) and I graduated on June 25, 2004, with a bachelor's degree and specialization in Christian Education.

While studying, however, I was asked to be part of a volunteer chaplaincy program to lead daily devotion and meditation at a nearby high school. It was a wonderful learning experience where I was able to provide pastoral care to teenagers and be present for their personal, familial, scholastic, and emotional issues.

Moreover, I was also a member of a chaplaincy prison ministry team. I must admit, at first, the experience was scary. I was scared entering that high security prison. Many negative thoughts went through my mind. I did not know what to expect or how to behave among those criminals in a small chapel during a worship service. I was extremely concerned about my safety.

I did not want to be a victim while ministering because many of them would have nothing to lose if they were to attack us. Candidly, I even questioned my decision to join that ministry team. To be blunt, I did not even feel comfortable closing my eyes during prayer time. To say the least, I was on high alert and ready to defend myself if something were to go wrong.

I also worked weekly with a local food bank and resource organization, Food for the Poor, to deliver weekly groceries to several ghetto communities and visited patients with HIV AIDS to provide pastoral presence, companionship, and comfort while listening to their stories. Sadly, their families had abandoned many of them because of their medical conditions.

Those experiences greatly shaped my ministry with those going through life's challenges. Looking back, I feel comfortable to say that those inmates and patients ministered to me, too. I was impressed by their apparent relationship with a higher power during some difficult, peculiar, and stressful situations.

When I began my graduate studies in the spring of 2006 at Campbell University Divinity School (CUDS), I did not know what my specialization was going to be. After wetting my feet during the first year, I began examining and reflecting on my journey thus far and noticed a pattern of chaplaincy experiences from 1995 to 2005.

As a result, I took some counseling classes, studied about major world religions, and met with the department chairperson about my interest in the chaplaincy field. I usually like to be well informed before engaging in anything.

Religious Quest - Islam and Jehovah's Witnesses

One of many lessons I learned is that having an open mind about all religious traditions and learning about them was essential in order to be an efficient, unbiased, and productive spiritual care giver. As a result, I embarked on a world religions quest by taking classes, visiting many religious communities throughout Wake County to learn and spend time with different religious leaders and parishioners. At the end of my pursuit, I specialized in Islam and Jehovah's Witnesses as they were and still are two of the most growing religious groups worldwide.

Learning about Islam

I spent six months visiting mosques, studying Islam, and its founder, Muhammad, ("Peace be upon him," as they say after mentioning his name). Islam is the second largest religion in the world after Christianity with 24.9% of the world population. I had the privilege to interview some Muslims, Imams, and observe countless worship services. An Islamic Friday worship observance, Dhuhr, is like a regular Sunday worship service in the Christian church tradition with a moment for preaching, or khutbah as they say in Islam.

Islam has two major denominations, Suni and Shia. However, due to major theological differences, traditions, and rituals between them, they do not worship together. Yet, even within the two denominations, there are many sectarian groups. Also, men and women are not allowed to congregate together during their worship services.

As a result, during my learning experience I took turns observing each gender's worship style. While visiting an Islamic community, I made a faux pas by extending my right hand to greet a Muslim lady and she literally refused and nodded as a sign to acknowledge my greeting. At first, I felt embarrassed and did not know what to do next, but later, I learned that Islamic women were not supposed to touch strangers' hands.

About five years later while working at a death row prison, a Muslim lady and I were members of an interdisciplinary group at the mental health unit. Later on, we became professionally and religiously comfortable with each other in asking questions, and she assisted me in learning more about Islam and vice versa.

Islamic children must learn Arabic, the Qur'an, and attend mainly Islamic schools, if possible, during their developmental years. Many of them can recite verses from their sacred book, the Qur'an, from memory. One day, I was allowed to interview a young boy, who was probably 10 or 12 years old.

I was impressed by his recollection when reciting those Qur'anic verses. Afterward, I asked him to explain those verses in English, and he could not. Minutes later, after an awkward moment of silence, one of the religious leaders asked him to go back to his classroom. I felt bad for him because it was not my intention to embarrass him when I asked that question. I thought he knew those sacred scriptural verses in English as well.

From that experience and more, I have come to conclude that, sometimes, reciting something does not necessarily equate to understanding. That experience was the result of indoctrination and not teaching, and the latter one requires comprehension with the skill to explain as needed. When a material, secular or religious, is understood, explaining it in many cases tends to come effortlessly.

Before I knew it, my journey into the Islamic world ended. It was a great opportunity to learn about their philosophy, theology, and evangelistic approach. After expressing my gratitude to the Islamic community, one of the leaders extended the invitation moving forward.

Witnessing Jehovah

The Jehovah's Witness organization was next on my religious quest to study with the hope to have a full grasp of their theology, traditions, religious philosophy and growth strategy because they are growing like a wildfire with 8.7 million adherents. Their main focus is door-to-door evangelism, and it seems to be working.

Due to their one-on-one approach, they have been affected greatly by the COVID-19 worldwide pandemic as they have been warned by their governing board not to go to people's houses. They, however, still meet via zoom with their current converts.

Annually, they have a memorial service to commemorate the death and resurrection of Jesus Christ, the founder of Christianity. Over seventeen million people usually attends that service

160

worldwide. I had the privilege to attend this memorial service during my religious inquiry. There is solemn reverence throughout the celebration. During that service, they also serve the Lord's Supper, which is a piece of bread and red wine or grape juice, which they hold once a year.

At the end of that memorial service, I noticed that not all the members, including the leader who was assigned to me, had partaken of those ritual items. I asked him for his reasoning for not partaking in the Lord's Supper. "I am not among those 144,000 elects," he responded.

Who are those elects? Jehovah's Witnesses believe that those faithful Christians from the day of the Pentecost, which most Christians consider as the Genesis of the Christian church, of thirty-three Anno Domini (AD), meaning in the year of our Lord, until the present day will be resurrected to heaven as immortal spirit beings to spend eternity with God and Christ. Hence, according to them these people have been chosen by God before the beginning of time, according to their interpretation of Revelation 14:1-4.

"Sir, may I ask you another question?" I asked. "How do you know you are not in the 'magic' number?" "Well! I just know." He answered. "If that is the case, don't you think you might be wasting your time because why bother if your name did make it on that special list?" "You raised a very good point, but one thing I can tell you is that I am not wasting my time." He said and shook my hand and told me, "See you next time!" to which I interpreted as a way of saying we were done here.

We met every two weeks for coffee to learn about his organization. By the way, he was an ordained Baptist deacon for years and became a Jehovah's witness because he claimed he found the truth. One day during lunch, he told me that unlike Baptist clergies, Jehovah's witnesses elders are volunteers. They do not believe in receiving a salary for doing God's work. I was impressed and speechless for a moment as I wondered about practical matters such as paying for family expenses, college, housing, food, transportation, and paying bills.

"Yes, I have a family with children. I live in a house with a mortgage, and everything else you questioned is paid for by the organization," he explained. "Really? I exclaimed with a puzzled look on my face." How and where can I sign up to be become a Jehovah's witness elder? I jokingly asked. Then, I said to him, with all due respect, "Sir, you are being paid. The money does not go through your hands, literally, but all your worries have been taken care of. You are financially better off than many religious leaders."

He went on with his comparison by saying that unlike Baptist churches, they do not pass plates during worship services to collect tithes and offerings because the organization does not believe in asking people for money.

I told him that the last time I was in one of the kingdom halls, it was clean, there was running water, we did not worship in darkness, the building was well air-conditioned and so on. So, where did you find money to keep this place so well kept?" I asked. "Well, we put a box at the entrance for people to give their tithes and offerings while someone is standing adjacent to keep an eye on the container." He explained. "Sir, it is evident that you still collect money, but you use a different approach." After a moment of debate, we both laughed.

Based on my research, you will never find someone who was born in that faith and tradition with a bachelor's degree or higher. They believe one needs to learn a simple trade to live by while waiting for Jesus to come back. Spending years in school is a waste of time and resources. However, those with higher educational degrees usually are the ones who had joined the organization.

Their door-to-door evangelism strategy pays off because they are one of the fastest growing religious groups. One of their strengths is that they do not take rejection personally. They have been trained to believe that is a small price to pay while winning souls for God. They are determined and well trained as I had observed their door-to-door evangelistic rehearsal.

Based on my religious investigation, you will never find a mega kingdom hall building, which is intentional in their approach. They are community minded. Therefore, having a large facility would diminish their communal objective to build bonds through relationships, which can be challenging to do in a larger context.

However, once a kingdom hall has almost reached its capacity, the local and governing leaders start their search to build another one in a different location. Also, they have no windows in their buildings because they do not want to be distracted by the outside world. Their building capacity limit was two hundred and fifty worshippers at that time.

During those six months of studying Jehovah's Witnesses theology, philosophy, and observing their worship services, I came to many conclusions, but the one that stood out the most was their dedication to their mission. It is a very well-structured institution like the Roman Catholics and the Seventh-day Adventist in terms of regulating all weekly materials that will be used worldwide. Case in point, during a worship service, any given religious materials, sacred or otherwise, has been chosen or selected by a governing body.

Consequently, parishioners will hear the same scripture passages or material presented no matter where they are around the globe. On the surface, it seems organized but at the same time the work of the Holy Spirit seems to be under control. Hence, local churches appear robotic and have no authority to be creative or independent. In other words, local leaders seem only qualified to read what has been prepared for them. I cannot help but wonder if it is because the governing body thinks that they are either not holy enough for Holy Spirit to use to them or the leadership board does not trust their intellect to think and plan a religious calendar.

I concluded my academic religious pursuit with them by attending a worship service at one of their kingdom halls. I thanked all the elders, and especially the one who was assigned to me for those six months and wished them all the best in their ministry.

"Edisson, I have one thing I want to say to you," The assigned leader stated. "So far, I have never met a person so tenacious like you." He declared. "What do you mean?" I asked. "Some students who come here to learn about us either end up becoming one of us or quite midway, but you completed everything and did not become a member. Frankly, I was hoping you would come to know Jehovah." He explained.

I looked at him, smiled, and thanked him for his observation. Then, I told him that I knew what I believed in long before I embarked in that religious quest. Therefore, joining another religious group would not make me closer to God, but it might improve my relationship with my religious like-minded people.

Moreover, I informed him that to know God means to develop an intimate relationship with Him, and it is personal. However, communal worship is also important in that process, but not number one. We both shook hands for the last time and departed.

It was a wonderful experience learning about some religious groups, visiting their communities, and interviewing those leaders as a group during a practicum as well as individually through my quest. At first, it was uncomfortable visiting certain sites but that was part of the learning curve. I will forever cherish those moments. At the end of those practica, I had the honor and privilege to work with the distinguished professor, Dr. George Braswell, in the World Religions department at Campbell University Divinity School. He has been considered the expert on world religions.

Internship and Residency

I did not know what to expect as a chaplain intern in a hospital. I will never forget on the first day when one of the supervisors told us about morgue duty. She gave us a tour of that huge hospital, which at that time had about one thousand beds. Then, she instructed us to come back at 1:00 PM after lunch to visit that hospital's morgue.

Upon returning, she informed us that one of the interns decided to quit the training because he said that going to the hospital morgue was a deal breaker for him. Of course, we did not know his previous experience. Looking back, I felt that being in a place with corpses could have trigged some past emotions and resulted in Post-Traumatic Stress Disorder (PTSD).

I must admit that many of us were not looking forward to visiting that morgue. Some complained that being around dead people was scary. "You should be only scared of the living and not the dead because they are harmless." Our supervisor told us.

Anyway, as interns, we were trained to take some grieving loved ones to that hospital morgue to say their goodbyes one more time before they left that hospital. Also, when there were stillborn babies, chaplains were the only ones (at that time) who could bring that miniature corpse wrapped in white linens to a grieving mother or father one more time before they were discharged. Like any training, there will be always some highs and lows especially during the initial learning season. From my experience and informal survey, it seems that the human brain may not be too comfortable with new knowledge. In that context, there seems to be a moment *of flight, freeze, and fight* when it comes to learning or stepping into an unfamiliar territory.

During the *flight* moment, a person might decide to quit without even trying simply because of an unchartered territory. The *freeze* part comes when a person has decided to embark on this new adventure even though she or he, at first, did not want to but decided to try it anyway. Suddenly, having realized that was a mistake, the person became frozen and took *flight* for good.

The learning *fight* stage is when we challenge our brain or others assist us to become used to that new adventure. Those of us who have children, for instance, can remember how some of them had struggled when they were learning to walk or ride a bicycle. Hence, how stressful it was for them when it was time to remove those training wheels one by one or at once from their ride by teaching them how to balance. Of course, none of us can forget the frightening experience of being behind the wheel of a car for the first time.

I can go on and on with life's examples when it comes to a learning adventure. The bottom line is to never give up during those first two responses because your brain will adjust to it because humans have the ability to do so. Remember, people do not become a master of anything over night! It takes some trials and tribulations before succeeding.

At the end of the summer of 2008, I completed my internship in chaplaincy in Raleigh and Zebulon, NC with the Spiritual Care Department at WakeMed Health and Hospitals. It was a great learning experience where I began to learn to be comfortable with sick and dying patients, listened actively, and with compassion while providing pastoral presence.

Time seemed to fly while I was learning. As I was busy completing my final research paper to graduate, I was accepted in the residency program at the same hospital where I completed my internship. Therefore, it was time to dive deeper into chaplaincy.

I was thrilled by that news and could not wait to start the residency program. I tied the knot the day after my graduation on Friday, May 14, 2010, where my new wife, Nelcie, and I were surrounded by caring and loving people. We went to Jamaica for our honeymoon. I spent about three months in my homeland because I wanted a break for my mental health after four years of tense graduate studies. During that time, we were able to build some emotional connection as newlyweds when she came back from work.

The residency was a one-year program, and residents are part of the emergency department team. One of our job's descriptions was to contact families if an individual was unable to do so after an accident. We were not allowed to share sad news with patients' family members because most people tend to associate a sad news deliverer with his or her ordeal. Afterward, providing pastoral support could be problematic. Chaplains are trained to provide pastoral support and not be sad news bearers.

At the end of a pastoral visit, a patient wanted to share something personal with me. He said that he was literally dying, and he and a lady had been in a cohabiting relationship for years with no children. He wanted to marry her so that she could inherit his estate. Later, I met with both of them and instructed them about what to do in terms of having the legal document I would need to officiate the wedding ceremony. After another chaplain and I met with them on several occasions for pre-marital counseling sessions, they officially became spouses. They were extremely grateful, especially, the wife. He died weeks later.

Being a resident in a chaplaincy program could be both challenging and rewarding because one had a year to foster a professional relationship, share, and debate some emotional issues, which was uncomfortable and emotionally painful at times.

A chaplain is an integral member in the Emergency Department (ED), and one must be present at the arrival of a patient. The first mistake I made on my initial on-call was when I told some staff members that it seemed quiet here. I was rebuked swiftly and was also told never to use the Q word, which was *quiet* because it was believed that might trigger business during a work shift. Consequently, one lady knocked on something, which meant for the quietness to remain as it was.

One day, two parents desired to see their stillborn for the last time before being discharged. As I was going to that hospital morgue to take a stillborn child to his parents, my beeper went off informing me of an ambulance in route to the emergency department with an estimated time of arrival of five minutes. Unable to be at both places at once, a colleague volunteered to take that stillborn baby to those parents on my behalf, which was genuinely nice of him.

Upon arriving at the ED, the patient was alert and oriented, and his wife was on her way. My chaplain's duty was concluded once that patient shared that information, and I did my documentation. Subsequently, I tried to contact that colleague who had gone to that morgue, but he had left his phone behind and did not receive my message.

As soon as he came back and saw me, he told me, "You sat here and let me do your job. You went to the ED and did nothing. I am angry with you." He was loud and clearly upset. As I was about to open my mouth to explain, he raised his voice louder and louder with hand gestures and said, I am mad and do not bother talk to me now."

Then, I urged him to calm down. "How dare you to ask me to calm down?" he shouted. Suddenly, I saw one of our supervisors passing by, and thought she was going to intervene, but she just passed through and said nothing. I was kind of disappointed by her silence because I hoped she would have inquired about the commotion.

Later that day, we were able to talk about the situation after the storm had passed. He told me that going to that hospital morgue to pick up a stillborn was always a painful experience for him because he and his wife had been trying to have a baby for years.

I also learned a valuable lesson to never tell someone who is angry to calm down. Making a statement like that tends to exacerbate a situation. Afterward, our supervisor came and applauded us for working things out between us and said that she intentionally chose not to say anything and allowed us to work through the conflict on our own.

Becoming and being a chaplain requires a deep theological foundation and understanding, personal faith, and a healthy self-esteem. Over the years, I have come to realize that a pastor is not a chaplain, but a chaplain is a pastor. Years ago, that was the case.

A well-trained chaplain provides pastoral care, and not religious care. A pastor, however, is trained to minister to his own theological like-minded people, while a chaplain's education is designed to minister to all people regardless of their religious faith traditions and cultures. In other words, chaplains are clergies without religious border.

A chaplain receives more extensive theological training than a pastor. For instance, someone in most churches can be the pastor of a local church after a four-year degree from a theological institution. To the contrary, having a master's degree, completing internship, and residency are required to be hired as a chaplain. Technically, it is about a ten-year process, and takes another two years to become board certified.

Religion and politics have one thing in common, they sometimes divide people. Consequently, many rather associate themselves with spirituality. It has a religious component in it, but it is not religion. It is bigger than religions. It is about self-discovery in all life's aspects. Many, sadly, use the two interchangeably.

Case in point, the late Tafari Makonnen a.k.a. Haile Selassie I, Emperor of Ethiopia, asserted, "Spirituality is not theology or ideology. It is simply a way of life, pure and original as given by the Most High. Spirituality is a network linking us to the Most High, the universe, and each other."[17]

---

[17] https://bit.ly/33ULpRd - Access date: 11.11.2021

Confronting Prejudice

While on-call, a high school senior was brought to that hospital after falling from a three-story building doing a backflip, which he had done numerous times with his friends. This time something went wrong, he fell on his head. His family migrated from Afghanistan and appeared to be very caring and welcoming people when I met them. After I introduced myself as the on-call chaplain, the father's friendly attitude changed and said with a firm voice, "We do not need you here. We are fine. You can leave." I told him I respected his decision, but before leaving I would check on them sporadically throughout the day until my shift ended.

The family room was filled with that young man's loved ones, relatives, fellow Muslims, high school staff, friends, and of course a secret girlfriend that his parents had no clue existed because they wanted him to date an Islamic lady. She was present and yet could not come too close to the family to avoid being questioned about her connection.

The father was convinced that his Islamic leaders could pray to Allah for a miracle to reduce the inflammation in his son's brain. I escorted them to the hospital chapel, provided them with some Islamic prayer rugs, and they spent hours praying.

Every hour or so, I checked on them if they had needed anything to drink or eat. Some of them requested water and some were escorted to the hospital's cafeteria or vending machine. I was able to meet many of their requests. During a briefing at the end of my shift, I informed the next chaplain of that critical and sad situation with that family, and he agreed to keep checking on them.

Two days later, I was informed that young man's father wanted to see me and said, "Chaplain, I owe you an apology for the way I have been treating you, and my vile behavior did not stop you from supporting me and my family. You are a true brother." Then, we hugged. He continued by adding, "My family and I would like you to be present when the medical team pulls the plug on my son.

Also, your presence would mean a lot to us at my son's funeral." I was able to meet his two requests.

While examining my training, I learned not to take what patients and families might say personally because their emotions are high. Going through a health crisis or caring for a family member may test someone in many ways unimaginable. I think people by nature are not rude. Certain circumstances, however, may turn them into something completely opposite of their personality.

Meaning of Trust

About three months into the residency, one of the chaplains, during a moment of fellowship, told me that he trusted me. "Okay?" I replied with a puzzled voice. After an awkward silence, He asked, "Do you trust me, too?" Candidly I told him, "I do not because trusting someone takes time, requires moments of camaraderie in different contexts, being vulnerable with one another, challenging one another, and sharing some high and low moments. Also, it could not happen within a few months. I only knew you within the chaplaincy context. I wish I could say the same about you. However, I would hope to trust you eventually." His attitude afterward indicated that he was not pleased with my answer.

Trust is more than a belief, and the latter one has to do with head knowledge rather than intimacy. Trust demands both faith and an intimate relationship with a certain level of honesty and vulnerability.

On the United Stated currency, for instance, it reads, "In God We Trust," which was signed by President Eisenhower on July 30, 1956, who declared the phrase to be the national motto after the eighty-fourth Congress passed that legislation. I wonder if that last word on the US national moto should be *believe* instead of *trust*. Could it be back then, those two words, trust and believe, were used interchangeably?

Anyway, after living in this great country for about sixteen years, I have been learning academically, socially, religiously, politically, and most importantly about the deep racial dynamics and their implications on almost some mundane activities. Unfortunately, many are being victimized while some are profiting from that system, as a result.

White Privilege

As an international student, I had to have an employment card before starting the chaplaincy training. Sixty days prior to its expiration date, as recommended by United States Citizenship Immigration Services (USCIS), I applied for another one, but it did not arrive on time.

Those of us who have had immigration cases with the USCIS would agree with the fact the service is not as fast as some would hope. Three months before the residency ended, a human resource representative from that hospital reminded me about my upcoming work expiration card, and I told her that a new one might arrive any day.

It was a stressful and challenging moment in my life because my wife and I were expecting our first son in the next three months. As my ordeal became the talk in the spiritual care department, one resident said, "Edisson, if you want I can take you to the human resource department, and they will let you finish the program without a new card. It is called white privilege." I was shocked and speechless after hearing that statement. Generally, I tend not to talk whenever I am disgusted or distraught. I usually take time to process and ponder a situation before sharing my feelings.

Twenty-four hours later, I sent him a lengthy email explaining how I felt about his insensitive statement as a pastoral care provider in training, and how disappointed and emotionally hurt I was when he used my ordeal to play the race card. He was apologetic in his reply and for his thoughtlessness toward my situation.

Looking back, I felt like that chaplain was making fun of my circumstance and in the process hurt my feelings. Late Maya Angelou was right when she said, "I've learned that people will forget what you said, people will forget what you did, but people will never forget how you made them feel."[18]

Wearing a Collar Sends Mixed Messages

Decades ago, ministry was associated with a local church only, and unfortunately, some people still have that mentality. In other words, anything beyond the walls of a local church is not considered ministry.

One day while on call, I made a post-surgery pastoral care visit to one of my patients, and her room was filled with families and friends. Consequently, I told her I would come back later before my shift ended and urged her to spend time with her visitors. As I was leaving, a gentleman asked, "Chaplain, can I talk to you outside?" He extended his right hand for a handshake and stated, "You are a life saver. You came at the right time. By the way, I am the patient's pastor, and I hate coming to hospitals to visit my parishioners. I have been in ministry for thirty-five plus years and have been struggling with that ministerial aspect." Then, he asked, "How do you do what you do, ministering in a hospital setting?"

"Before I answer you, can I ask you something, too? How do you do what you do, being a pastor of a local church for more than thirty-five years where the attention is on you every Sunday?" I asked. "Oh! I see now! It is about your calling," he answered with a smile. "Exactly!" I replied. Then, we both thanked each other for our ministries.

Whenever I was on-call, I wore my clerical collar to avoid introducing myself to patients and loved ones. One afternoon, a

---

[18] https://bit.ly/3JblHbh - Access date: 8.10.2021

bicyclist was brought to the emergency room after being hit by a car, and thankfully he was okay, but I had to follow protocol by asking him if he would like me to inform a family member.

As soon as I entered his room, he anxiously said, "Wait a minute! Am I dying? I thought the medical team told me that I was okay and ready to be discharged. Why did they send a chaplain?" "Sir, first of all, you are not dying. I am just here to check on you and to find out if you need me to inform a family member to come to pick you up." I explained. Then, I asked why he thought he was dying as soon as he saw me? "According to Hollywood movies, chaplains usually visit dying patients. As soon as I saw your clergy shirt, I was freaked out, thinking that the doctor had lied to me," he explained. We both had a good laugh about the situation and concluded how Hollywood could influence our perspective on certain things.

Coming Full Circle

Being on-call for twenty-four hours in any hospital was unpredictable. Sometimes there were no emergencies, and other cases, it was like rush hour traffic. No matter how each shift ended, class started at 8:00 AM the next day after briefing that next on-call person and the pastoral care team.

One day, my on-call beeper beeped while in class. I was informed not to come to the emergency department but instead to send my supervisor. I told the person on the other end of the line that I was on duty and that was my responsibility and not my supervisor's. "Chaplain, I understand, but I am requesting your supervisor and not you," she firmly reiterated. "That is odd! In my decades working here, I have never received such request." My supervisor who was also teaching that class gave us something to do and left. As she was leaving, I jokingly told her that I hoped the rest of my shift could go like that. She looked at me and said, "Wishful thinking, Edisson!"

One hour later, we were informed that our spiritual care director collapsed in that hospital's parking lot and died. The hospital administration and employees from other departments came to provide support and comfort throughout that day and beyond.

Ten years later, I visited one of my patients while working as a spiritual care counselor with a wonderful hospice organization, Transitions LifeCare, Raleigh, NC. During our initial conversation, as we were building some rapport with the hope to understand her spiritual journey better, she told me that she was an emergency nurse at WakeMed Health and Hospitals in Raleigh for years; and also, she was not religious.

Subsequently, I told her that humans are on a spiritual quest, and my goal was not to provide religious care but rather spiritual one because religions tend to divide people. Spiritual care, on the other hand, has to do with self- discovery and understanding every aspect of one's life in relationship with a higher power. In other words, each life's circumstance, should be considered as a teaching moment that gears toward making us better rather than bitter in our spiritual journey.

Anyway, after listening to some of her personal and professional stories, I asked some questions about her tenure at that hospital emergency department and shared mine. Surprisingly, it was concluded that she was that same person who told me to send my supervisor at the emergency department the morning I was on-call. She recalled that conversation as if it were yesterday.

Then, I asked her to explain her reasoning for not wanting me to come to the ED because I wanted to know. "As an ED nurse for years, I learned to make split-second decisions, and concluded it would have been too much for a trainee to see his director in such condition." I thanked her for being considerate and professional even during a time of crisis. Weeks later, she died.

Chaplaincy and storytelling go hand-in-hand. If one does not like to listen to stories, becoming a chaplain might not be a good fit. Active listening is crucial in the process in order to begin understanding that person and make a positive impact during a pastoral relationship. It also involves paying attention to details and asking open-ended questions. Sometimes some between-the-line answers and questions could be cues in connecting the dots, which should help in the understanding process without being biased or judgmental.

Overall, the internship and the residency challenged me in ways I never thought possible in all aspects in my life, and most importantly in being present and learning to be comfortable with people who were going through life's challenges within the American context. I will forever cherish those trainings because they shaped me tremendously. At the end, one of the trainees described that training as "Boot Camp for Ministers."

Chapter Thirteen
Serving Time in a Juvenile Facility

I never thought in a million years that I would start my official chaplaincy career in a juvenile facility also called Youth Development Center, but that was how it all began. I completed my residency as a chaplain three days before my wife and I became parents. It was the worst time for someone to be out of a job. I had many interviews during the end of my residency and hoped to start working once I completed the program; but things did not go as planned.

As a result, I began my greatest dream, fatherhood as a jobless parent. My wife and I had to make ends meet with unemployment benefits while job hunting. After co-parenting for three months and several interviews, with no job, I volunteered with a local non-profit organization, Urban Ministry in Raleigh, NC.

I chose to volunteer because it was almost impossible to spend eight hours a day job hunting. Each day I devoted six hours to volunteering and two hours hunting for chaplaincy jobs in NC. I realized that starting a chaplaincy career in my state seemed difficult, and so I extended my search nationwide.

We were ready and determined to go anywhere. At one point, I even considered talking to a friend in the construction business to work as a sub-contractor or find something in a restaurant in the meantime. I did not feel comfortable receiving weekly unemployment benefits.

After being jobless for almost a year, I had two chaplaincy job offers; one in south Florida with a Baptist hospital, and the other one with the North Carolina Juvenile Justice System at a male facility. We decided to stay here because it would have been too much to move to Florida with an infant.

I was thrilled to find a job and nervous at the same time because I was going to work with juveniles and did not know what to

177

expect. Nevertheless, I was determined and ready for the new professional challenge. I spent several weeks building rapport with juveniles, employees, and volunteers in order to learn about the working culture as well as about those teenagers' temperaments, attitudes, and behaviors from their peers and employees.

I sat in several classes (which took place inside the center with correctional officers providing security), joined them during lunch time, took part in social activities, and of course supervised religious worship services.

They began opening up and started asking me questions or sending formal requests to meet for pastoral counseling. I met with them in groups and one-on-one, but always in a place where there were working video cameras.

Some of them asked me about my personal life and I did not respond. I told them that I was there to build a professional relationship and not a friendship. Hence, I would like to keep my private life private. Most of them agreed and respected that decision.

They wanted to know my faith tradition and requested a question-and-answer session where they could learn more about my religion and other ones. Weeks after answering their questions, some of them expressed a desire to be baptized like the founder of Christianity, Jesus Christ.

I asked them to make a formal request and said I would talk to the facility director to find out about the policy and the Standard of Operating Procedures (SOPs) for having a water baptismal service by immersion on campus. As minors, they would also need written permission from their parents or guardians. Therefore, letters were mailed for consent and only one parent declined.

Using Juveniles for Publicity

We spent about eight weeks teaching the history of water baptism, its significance, and its purpose. At the end of the session, all of them wanted to proceed with the religious ritual. In the meantime, I was busy looking for a portable baptistry to perform the baptismal service. Through a staff connection, I met with a local pastor who agreed to lend us one. I was excited and ready to select a date for the service.

Suddenly, the local pastor said, "Chaplain, there is one condition on your using the portable baptistry. You will have to allow a local newspaper to attend the baptismal service and write an article." I told him that would be impossible because the children were in state custody, but I would share his request with the facility director, and they rejected his request.

After informing that local pastor of the facility director's decision, he told me that he would not be able to loan us the portable baptistry anymore. I thanked him and left with the hope he would have a change of heart and call me, but I was wrong. His requirements left a bad taste in my mouth because he seemed to be more concerned about using the juveniles to publicize his ministry.

As a result, I was back to square one and we were less than two weeks away. Therefore, I decided to reach out to a local church and share my predicament with its leaders. They made their sanctuary available for the water baptismal service at no cost and with no obligations; they also included their reception hall. One valuable lesson I have learned is that blessings can be right in front of us, and we are busy looking for them elsewhere. That church not only allowed us to use their built-in baptistry but also provided white garments for the youth to wear on their special day.

With less than two weeks before the ceremony, one of the baptismal candidates changed his mind about getting baptized. When I asked him the reason for his change of heart, he suddenly became sad and said, "My best friend drowned in a lake days before my arrest, and I am concerned the same thing may happen to me while going under the water during the baptismal service." I expressed my condolences, provided some pastoral comfort, and told him that I respected his decision. After further pastoral counseling sessions, he agreed to be baptized by affusion, the pouring of water over his head instead of being fully submerged.

To my surprise, the facility management, per policy and SOPs, wanted the youth to be handcuffed and shackled while in the baptismal pool for safety and security reasons. After much debate with them, the baptismal candidates were allowed to be baptized without them.

When it was time for the juvenile with the Post Traumatic Stress Disorder (PTSD) to come into the water, he whispered into one of my ears and said, "Chaplain, I am ready to go under the water completely." I looked at him with a smile of agreement and baptized him.

Everything went well, as anticipated. Some parents and guardians were in attendance, and some even became emotional. They expressed their gratitude for the opportunity to be present. With the assistance of staff and volunteers, we even had a reception afterward. The baptismal commission contributed greatly to that joyful event. It was indeed a team effort.

Closing and Moving

About seven months later, I was transferred to a co-ed facility, which was about an hour and a half drive. The government had closed down that five-year-old state of the art facility, which I thought was a waste of taxpayers' money and a lack of pro-active leadership. Then, that facility was reopened less than three years later.

American families, especially brown ones, have been impacted negatively by the prison system. As a result, children have been raised and continue to be raised by grandparents and caring strangers (through government programs) while their parents are incarcerated.

For some families, the prison system is the only life they have known. Therefore, it has become like a generational curse for some. One of the juveniles, for instance, told me that his biological mother was his neighbor. "What do you mean by that?," I asked. He told me that his mom was serving time at the women's prison, which was less than five minutes, walking distance, from our facility. Frankly, I did not know what to say. He told me that in three years he had lived with four different families before he ended up in prison.

Some people cannot help but repeat what they have been exposed to. Therefore, it is crucial for parents to be intentional with some of the things they are exposing their children to. Values are not taught but seen. Children do what they see and not what they hear.

During a counseling session, one juvenile girl told me how much she hated men. I asked her to unpack that statement. She refused. As we continued talking, I began asking her about her upbringing and relationships with her parents. "Chaplain, I will never forget the day I watched my father packing his stuff in a suitcase, and that was the last time I saw him. I was eight years old when he left my mom and I," she explained.

"As an eight-year-old, how did you feel?" I asked. "Unloved! Abandoned! Sad! As a result, I do not like men. I am sorry for including you in that category because you seem to be a nice man trying to assist us while in prison," she revealed. I assured her that was okay, she had a right to feel that way and I would never blame or judge her.

She continued, "Months after my father left us, I watched men come and go; they never stayed long. Some of them even abused my mom physically and I could hear her crying while in my room."

She paused and began crying. I inquired if she was okay. Her soft reply was, "Talking about it felt like those things happened yesterday." I reassured her that it was okay to cry, once again. Then, I asked her if any of those men had finally developed a long-term emotional relationship with her mom. She responded, "No. The longest relationship lasted only six months."

"Weeks later, my mom began an intimate relationship with a woman, she became incredibly happy, and that woman never hurt or left her. Since my father's departure, it was the first time I saw my mom being herself," she explained.

Subsequently, she concluded that in order to be happy and not get hurt, she would stay away from men. Then, she told me, "That is why I only date girls even though some of the teenage boys here like me."

In the course of her prison sentence, we had developed a healthy chaplain-mentee relationship and she became comfortable sharing some personal stories during counseling sessions. About three months later, she was released.

Reaching Out with Compassion

Life is unpredictable. Most parents' wish is for their children to bury them and not the other way around. Unfortunately, for some parents in Newtown, Connecticut, that wish was shattered by a senseless shooting in one of their local schools, Sandy Hook Elementary School, on December 14, 2012.

It was a sad day for the great state of Connecticut and the nation. It was emotionally painful to watch innocent children and staff lose their lives for no reason and survivors overwhelmed with grief and emotions.

Our juveniles did not want to remain quiet during that dreadful event. They wanted to reach out to those survivors through letters, drawings, get well and thinking-of-you cards. Within days, the whole facility was busy working on those projects.

We were able to mail an enormous package to that grieving community to tell them that a juvenile facility in NC was thinking about them and praying for their families during that tragic and emotional moment.

Giving Back

Through several spiritual counseling sessions, I shared with them the value of giving back to one's community. As a result, on several occasions, we took some of them to some local churches that had a soup kitchen ministry and waited on those who came to eat, assisting with the clean-up afterward.

Through some wonderful volunteers, those teenagers in their free time learned how to crochet and make distinct items, including blankets. During the fall season, we would take them to local nursing homes or the Ronald McDonald House, in Chapel Hill, NC, a place for seriously ill children's parents to stay during surgery. At these places, they were able to donate those blankets for warmth and comfort.

I will never forget the excitement and pride in those juveniles' faces during those trips; and the grateful smiles of the people receiving their gifts. All of them confessed that it was a great feeling to accomplish something and then give it away to vulnerable people in our society.

During my tenure, I have realized that humans have the capacity to learn good or bad behaviors, but it all depends on the environment in which those individuals are evolving. No matter the crisis we face, we must keep learning and instilling values into the next generation.

Kids for Cash!

Based on my observation and experiences, the juvenile justice system in any society is the manifestation of an unstable family unit. Eight out of ten juveniles I worked with came from a broken home, (meaning there was something dysfunctional among members of that unit). Whenever that happens, there is room for chaos and that is when the slow slip begins, which eventually leads to misbehavior at homes, in the neighborhoods, in their school, and eventually, the involvement of the justice system.

One juvenile had been in and out of the system several times, better known as a frequent flyer. His parents were well educated, a medical doctor and a lawyer, and doing extremely well financially. During a pastoral counseling session, he told me, "I like being arrested, Chaplain." I asked him what he meant by that. He explained, "Since the divorce of my parents, the only time I see them together, without them yelling at each other, is when they come to bail me out at a police station."

Then, he told me that his mother and father were good providers but terrible parents. They would buy him expensive gifts to fill the void of never having time for him. As far as he could remember, he never saw them talking calmly, just arguing and yelling. He said that he used to think he was the source of their problems and wanted to run away.

Unfortunately, due to the dysfunctionality within some families, some people are taking advantage of those situations. Our society may never know the long-term negative impact the justice system will have on individuals.

I think some youngsters would not have gone through the system if their family was strong and better equipped in raising and discipling children. Unfortunately, some people are becoming richer through that brokenness.

Case in point, in August 2012, a former Pennsylvania juvenile judge, Mark Ciavarella Jr, took one million dollars in bribes from a building company in return for filling two detention centers with juveniles. He was later found guilty and sentenced to twenty-eight years in prison. The case was called "kids for cash!"

According to an article, "Ciavarella, was known for his harsh and autocratic courtroom demeanor, filled the beds of the private lockups with children as young as 10, many of them first-time offenders convicted of petty theft and other minor crimes."[19]

There are some bad apples in every organization or system. Locking children up, however, for financial gain is a new low in our society. Due to the love of money, humanity is fading away slowly in our society. Nowadays, some people want to become richer faster, and they do not care how that is done.

During a family trip, one of my sons asked me how old was the youngest child that I had worked with when I was a juvenile chaplain. "It was "a nine-year-old boy," I replied. "Nine? That's heartbreaking!" He bewildered. Then, he stated, "That boy should have been home with his parents."

My job as juvenile clinical chaplain sometimes went beyond providing spiritual care. I had accompanied many juveniles in attending the funerals of a parent or grandparent. There was a list of boxes that needed to be checked to guarantee safety and security in the surrounding area before planning any trip.

Hence, I spent countless hours practicing scenarios that required some proactive and reactive thinking. I encouraged them to use that method in almost all situations especially when hanging out with peers. Some "friends" sometimes would ask you to do something or follow even though they kind of knew there were illegal risks. Leaders think proactively before they do and follow. I reminded them that they were leaders, too, and it was okay to say no to some people after proactively assessing a request.

---

[19] https://bit.ly/3plxJH2 - Access date: 9.11.2020

Also, I challenged them to put their thoughts on paper daily or weekly through journaling. Therefore, I told them it was a good habit to put their feelings and thoughts on paper, which would help them to process a situation from a different angle. I chose that approach with them because writing could be a therapeutic tool especially for those who had experienced some traumas.

Getting Some Fast-Food

One day, after taking a young lady to attend her father's funeral service, and minutes after leaving, she informed us that she was starving. I must admit that the funeral service was long. It was almost a two-hour drive one way and she had already consumed her government issued snack. Per policy, we were allowed to buy lunch from any fast-food restaurant if a juvenile was hungry during a prolonged trip.

After talking to the assigned officer, I informed her that we would stop at the next exit to buy food. Once we pulled into a Burger King parking lot, she suddenly said, "I am no longer hungry." She apologized for wasting our time and we hit the road back.

Deep in my heart, however, I felt like she was not being truthful with us. "Is everything okay because earlier you told us that you were starving? Be frank with me." I kindly asked. "Sir, you took me by surprise when you told the officer to pull into that Burger King because I am a blood gang member." She explained. "What does Burger King have to do with gang activities?" I naively questioned. "For us, blood gang members, BK means blood killers. Only our rivals, Crips, would eat at a BK restaurant." She explained.

After listening to her explanation, it took me a minute to process the whole situation and I tried to put myself in her shoes to understand her. Later, she thanked us for taking her to another fast-food restaurant.

Exploring Life Beyond the Walls

One of my great joys as their chaplain was to watch some of those teenagers discovering who they were and what they could become through different tailored programs, social and religious activities. Many of them had almost no social skills or etiquette.

With the facility director's blessing, we were allowed to take some of those juveniles to visit different churches in town once a month. That was a great incentive based on good behavior with no write ups for the month prior.

Through the office of the chaplaincy, we received clothes donations because we wanted them to look nice whenever we were taking them out for any social event. We always made sure they wore nice civilian clothes and looked presentable. Our philosophy was to treat each juvenile with respect and dignity while they were incarcerated. Another one of our focuses was self-love and respect, while loving and respecting others.

Anyway, with no expectation of them doing so, the religious leaders offer lunch afterward. During debriefings, many of them confessed it was during those social activities that they learned how to behave properly in public. Others also said that it was their first time eating around a dining table without being involved in a fight over who would finish first or take the most food.

The world does not stop when one person is going through a life crisis. Attending classes while serving time was not optional for those juveniles. They attended classes five days a week. Many of them, as a result, were able to complete their General Educational Development (GED), which is equivalent to a high school diploma. I was fortunate enough to be present at some of those graduations. There was a sense of accomplishment when they received their diploma.

We decided to have a prom for those enrolled in that program as an incentive to motivate them to complete their courses and graduate as most of them would never have that experience. They studied extra hard with the hope to attend the prom gala. Prom dresses were donated as well as other items to make the event as real, formal, and exciting as possible for those juveniles. It was a team effort, and we had a remarkable success. In the end, each participant was extremely appreciative.

One of the things we observed was that many of those juveniles had poor table manners. As a result, we taught a class on dining etiquette. We practiced countless times how to use table utensils, the proper way to sit, what to do if they needed an item that was across the table, what to say if one needed to leave the table to use the bathroom, the proper way to belch, and to remember to express gratitude to the person/people who prepared that meal.

At the end of our class, many of them confessed that it was their first time learning those things. We, also, had faced some resistance from some of them who wanted to quit because learning those things was hard. It was like the flight theory I mentioned in the previous chapter.

People are indeed the products of their environment. Most of us tend to repeat what we have been exposed to in terms of unacceptable or acceptable behaviors. Those teenagers were able to exemplify a number of great social skills at the end of that refined environment.

While examining my time with those juveniles and beyond, I have concluded that values seem to have greater positive impact when they are being exhibited rather than taught. Also, being less judgmental in the process would help learners to be more comfortable when making mistakes during the learning process. Failure plays an integral part while studying. Those who do not want to fail will never learn.

The Price of Exhaustion

I used to drive one hour and thirty minutes one way to work. By the time I arrived home, ate dinner, and spent time with my family, it was time to take a shower, and retire to bed, in order to leave home the next morning at 5:45.

Several months later, I began feeling the physical and mental fatigue of being on the road roughly three hours a day. Additionally, filling up my vehicle's tank every two days was troublesome. I was denied a government vehicle to use for work, even though I knew other employees were using them.

After praying and talking to my wife about the whole situation and my wellbeing, my supervisor allowed me to work ten hours a day, four days a week, and I rented a local lodge. It was a blessing and a mixed feeling because I missed seeing my family every day.

Weeks later, my oldest son did not want to approach me when I arrived home on Thursday evening and would begin warming up toward me by Saturday morning. It seemed that he was missing me. Sadly, I had to leave home sometimes late Sunday evening or in the early hours Monday morning.

Working with the NC criminal justice system also meant all staff members must be certified. As a result, I spent four weeks in a police academy receiving rigorous training on how to defend myself in the event something was to go wrong. Thankfully, I never had to use my training on any juvenile.

Though I thoroughly enjoyed working with the youth, I started job hunting for something closer to home because I felt like I was missing some important milestones in my first son's life.

My professional goal was to be with the juvenile justice system until retirement, but I did not like my current situation. My wife and I thought about moving to that town but found that they did not have a good school system.

My goal has been and still is to put my family first, after God, in all my endeavors. It means nothing to me if I excel in my professional life and my family suffers during that time. Frankly, I would feel like a failure if that were to happen.

My ministerial pyramid has three layers, God, family, and ministry. Some clergies, on the other hand, put their loved ones at the bottom instead. As a result, many of them experience emotional breakdowns, suffer depression, experience instability or chaos in their home, and they are eventually filled with remorse at the end.

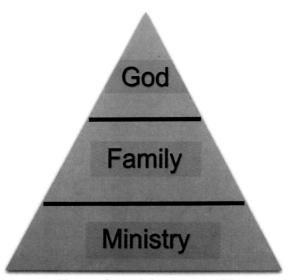

Picture of my ministerial pyramid

The opportunity to work with God's people is sacred and important, as a shepherd. Ministering to one's family, however, should be the utmost importance because ministers can be replaced but parents cannot. Remember, building lasting memories with loved ones is priceless. However, most faith organizations would start a replacement process, as soon as possible, because life continues. The world will remain with or without you.

Working with those juveniles was a terrific opportunity to assist in their self-discovery process and helping them develop a proactive skill when it came to decision making. It was a wonderful privilege because their brain was not fully developed. I hoped it was not too late for them to try a new acceptable lifestyle and stick with it.

Who is in Your Circle?

In the midst of everything, my wife and I became pregnant with our second son, which increased my urgency to be closer to my family. I increasingly placed importance on house chores, spending more time with our oldest child during that transitional period.

The phone signal in the place where I spent those four days was poor. After work, I would stay on the front porch relaxing and chatting with my wife and our oldest son until bedtime. At that time, unfortunately, there was no facetime feature or zoom. Now looking back, I felt like I was living in the dark ages.

One evening at about six o'clock, my wife informed me that our nephew was running around the house, accidentally pushed her, she fell, and an ambulance was on its way to take her to the nearest hospital. That was the worst phone call I had ever received. That nephew was in NC for an eye surgery with his mother, my biological sister, and we were hosting them.

I attempted to call my pastor but remembered he was at church for Wednesday's activities. I called the first neighbor, late Mr. Neal Newhouse, I met him and his wife, Elizabeth (who later became like my next-door parents through their love and care), days after I moved into the studio apartment in March 2006, he told me he was at one of his grandchildren's birthday parties and was ready to go be with my wife. I told him to wait and let me call someone else because I did not want to take him away from his loved ones.

Within seconds, I called my former graduate school carpool buddy, Reverend Andre Turrentine, he left his yard work unfinished and went straight to the hospital to be with my wife until I arrived. Then, I updated Mr. and Mrs. Newhouse and thanked them for their willingness to assist. Soon after, I headed to that local hospital.

After finding my wife in the emergency department and getting a good understanding of what was going on, I thanked my colleague, Andre, for coming so promptly and told him that he could leave. "Bro, I am not going anywhere until everything is over," he said. We all left the hospital about midnight, after all the tests revealed that my wife and our baby were fine.

While examining that situation, I concluded that crises, small or big, can reveal a lot about us in terms of how we manage them and how they affect us. Our mental calculation, as well as our human connection, can also determine the outcome of those crises.

Whether we realize it or not, our friendships and relationships with people can be summed up into three categories, circle, inner circle, and mini circle. Someone can be in all three. Certain people in the first circle, however, are there because of our shared Deoxyribo Nucleic Acid (DNA), and at times we may wish otherwise.

I believe any encounter in our journey has the potential to turn into a relationship and friendship. It all depends on those involved. Any human connection has a potential to grow or die. Therefore, both parties should be intentional in the nurturing process. Long lasting relationship will only endure tests of time if reciprocated both ways.

When it comes to the other two circles, however, it is up to us to decide who we invite in. Moving someone from one circle to the next should be based on a deeper level of experiences rather than emotional ones because our emotions may, sometimes, fail us.

The main difference among those three circles is their sizes in terms of who the insiders are. Also, the last two circles require certain level of trust and that does not build overnight. Those two should have people that are dependable and trustworthy.

During my family disaster, for example, I had to filter mentally my friendship list before calling anybody. This mental exercise should be swift because time is of the essence. In a crisis, if you are having difficulties finding names, it might be time to reassess your circles.

Case in point, within the life of the founder of Christianity, Jesus Christ, during what I call "his last will and testament on the cross," he designated one of his eleven disciples, John, to care for his mother, Mary, upon his death. "When Jesus saw his mother there, and the disciple whom he loved [within this context, the writer was referring to John] standing nearby, he said to her, "Woman, here is your son," and to the disciple, "Here is your mother." From that time on, this disciple took her into his home."[20]

Caring for someone's family member in any society could be considered as one of the highest honors and no one should take it lightly. To be given such responsibility is a sign of trust and moral character that the person has displayed throughout, which results in a closeness and confidence.

During my wife's emergency, I came to one conclusion, my mini circle has a few trusted friends. Assessing, categorizing, and examining a friendship mentally into those three circles through a

---

[20] John 19:26-27, NIV

potential crisis is a good exercise. That should help you to have a better understanding, in general.

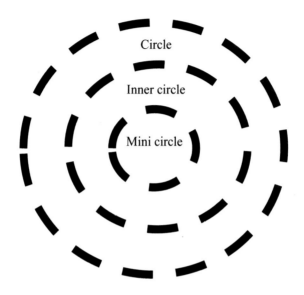

Explanation:

1.   The Circle: It can have as many people as you wish.

2.   **The Inner Circle:** It should have fewer people than the first one.

3.   **The Mini Circle:** It must only include best friends or trustworthy and dependable individuals.

Nota Bene: During that process, however, you may find yourself moving some people around based on your firsthand experiences with them. Also, the circles are broken, which means you have the power to remove anybody without informing that person.

Chapter Fourteen

Serving Time in a Death Row Prison

When I began my chaplaincy career in a juvenile facility, I never thought it would end in about two years to go deeper into the North Carolina Department of Public Safety division of adult correction in a death row penitentiary. That prospect would have never crossed my mind even in my wildest dream, but sometimes we just need to leave some room for surprises in our professional career.

I first met a maximum-security inmate on his dying hospital bed at WakeMed Health and Hospitals in Raleigh, NC during my residency. Families were not allowed to visit hospitalized inmates, but his wife had requested a hospital chaplain visit with him. I was present while he was transitioning as was his wife's wish.

Working with those juveniles put a strain on my young family relationship because I used to drive daily about three hours a day and fill up my car tank every two days. Then, I worked ten hours a day and four days a week in order to have a long weekend. After almost 2 years, I applied at an adult maximum-security prison for a clinical chaplain position.

After turning in my resignation letter, the facility manager told me that he did not see that coming and was speechless. Then, he warned me by saying, "Edisson, working at a maximum-security prison where there are death row inmates is extremely dangerous. I would hate for something terrible to happen to you. Nevertheless, I have to respect your decision." After listening, I thanked him for his concern and told him that something terrible could happen to me anywhere, even in that facility. "You are right," he replied. Then, he asked, "What can we do in order to change your mind about leaving us?" I told him that there was absolutely nothing because I already made up my mind for the sake of my family.

Two weeks later, I started a new chapter at that death row prison. It was about one hour round trip from home, which was a blessing compared to my previous place of employment. It was a great feeling to go home, daily, even though it took my oldest son a minute to get used to seeing me that much (but that was worth it, too).

I was disappointed to find out that I was considered as an internal transfer; therefore, there would be no salary negotiation even though my caseload would be eight times more. After looking at the pros and cons in terms of family time vis-à-vis reduction in commute, I accepted the offer, and three weeks later, I reported for duty.

Money can never replace family time even though some people tend to think that buying their children gifts can substitute their presence. I am yet to see adults who wished their parents had bought them more toys when they were children.

Upon arriving at the prison's lobby, I was asked to remove my belt before going through a scanner, and I had to step back because there was a "beep" suggesting that I still had a metal on me. I went through the scanner two more times before I found out that my shoes were the source. I had to place my shoes in a tray, so they could be examined carefully. Afterward, I was escorted to a conference room for new employees' orientation.

On my way, I noticed that all of the metal doors were controlled electronically by someone, somewhere else. I did not like that feeling because someone had the power to let an individual in or out in his or her own time.

That prison used to have six chaplains for six units. Before I joined their chaplaincy service in October 2013, the North Carolina state legislators had slashed that number in half, due to budget cuts. As a result, each chaplain was assigned to two units.

After I started working at that death row prison, my wife gave birth to our second son. Following my return from paternity leave, several inmates from my two assigned units wanted to know about my wife and the new baby's wellbeing. Upon asking them the source of that information, I was informed by all of them that my supervisor had told them.

I was unhappy not with those offenders but with my supervisor. He took the liberty to share my personal information in a maximum-security prison without my permission. Upon asking him about the whole situation, he simply told me that he did not think that was important. After listening to me, I respectfully told him that I would appreciate moving forward if I could make that decision because that was my story and not his.

During my professional career, I have been doing my best to keep my private life at home. Some colleagues, unfortunately, may use one's personal stories and use it as ammunitions in due time in the event something goes wrong with that relationship to hurt someone emotionally or otherwise.

Hearing a Familiar Name

I was assigned to two units, death row and general population. I told my supervisor that it was not fair to be assigned to the death row population as a chaplain coming from a juvenile facility.

"Chaplain, nobody will know it is your first time working in an adult prison unless you divulge that information. Also, those death row inmates are the most respectful ones," he explained. I looked at him and chuckled about that statement in disbelief.

Leading a weekly Christian Bible study for offenders of that faith tradition was one of my tasks. Inmates were to write their names and prison numbers legibly on a sheet of paper, for security and accountability purposes, before starting.

Strangely, while going through that list, one particular last name caught my attention and I asked to see that person afterward. One may wonder, "What is so special about a last name?" From my experience, some family names are unique and sometimes difficult to forget. That was the case with that person. My concern was if I knew him personally or professionally, per policy I had to report that to my direct supervisor and fill out some paperwork.

"Is everything okay, Chaplain?" he asked. I told him everything was fine and inquired if I knew him from somewhere. "I do not think so, this is the first time I am seeing you," he replied. "For some reason, your last name sounded familiar and that was my motive for asking," I revealed.

After asking him some personal questions, voilà, mystery solved. That man's oldest son was serving time at one of the juvenile facilities where I had previously worked. Unexpectedly, he became quiet and said, "I must change my life for the better and begin setting up good examples for my children. Chaplain, this meeting is a wake-up call and very eye-opening for my criminal activities. I just realized that my son is trying to be just like me," he somberly said.

Without planning, that encounter turned into a pastoral counseling session, and we met numerous times, upon his request, to further discuss some personal and familial issues. Throughout those sessions, there was a degree of remorse for past bad choices he had made as well as some destructive behaviors, which consequently impacted his family negatively.

Death Row Prisoners Are People, Too!

I was responsible for providing chaplaincy care to two units but was available to provide support at other units if their assigned chaplain was on vacation. One of my units was death row. I questioned my supervisor for sending me to that unit as a new chaplain, in a maximum-security prison. "Those offenders do not know it is your first time in a penitentiary," was his assurance.

I was scared to death. I did not know what to expect from "those murderers." The worst part was that my office was located on that unit; therefore, there was no way to avoid seeing them or meeting with them for various religious services. I wondered if my old job was still vacant so that I might call my former supervisor to go back.

I spent some time grieving my decision to leave the juvenile justice system where there were no death row inmates to deal with. However, seeing my family daily brought me joy. During those early days, I did everything I could to avoid being near the inmates. I spent most of my time in the general population building pastoral relationships with staff and residents. I only went to the other unit if and when I had to supervise a religious service, or an inmate requested to see me, or inform inmates the death of a family member to which at that time they would receive a telephone call for emotional closure.

I did not see how I was going to deal with men who murdered people for several hours a day. After pondering the situation, I concluded that going back to the youth development center was not an option because I must be home, daily, to help with house chores; especially, to help with the new addition in the family. I further came to my senses and realized that it could have been me on that unit waiting to be executed.

The last option was to change my attitude toward those men and focus on supporting them spiritually because, after all, it was my job. After assessing all my alternatives, I chose the latter one. It is amazing how a change in attitude can alter and determine the outlook of someone's demeanor toward other individuals we deem less human or inferior.

While examining my first trimester in that maximum-security prison, I decided I needed to change my attitude toward those death row offenders if I was to minister to them. After all, I was being paid, and most of all, I could not keep avoiding them forever. Most of all, those death row inmates are people, too.

Human beings have the potential to be discriminatory and judgmental toward people who might be different than us, or who have made some poor decisions and as a result serve time in a penitentiary. An unexamined self and motive might lead to self-importance and pride while putting others down.

Having said that, I printed that unit roster alphabetically and began seeing each inmate one by one. I would go to the recreation yard just to be with them outside a pastoral context. I told all of them that I was here to build a pastoral relationship with them and, in order to accomplish that goal, I had to spend time with them in order to know them as human beings.

During my tenure in the North Carolina justice system, I never had any interest in reading offenders' crime reports because I did not want any information to hinder my pastoral relationship with incarcerated juveniles and adults. Some of them asked if I read their crime report before meeting with them. I told them I had not because knowing what they did had nothing to do with providing pastoral support. However, if they chose to tell me, that was up to them.

One of them told me that he was on death row for a crime he did not commit. He told me that he was arrested, accused, tried, and convicted when he was nineteen years old while visiting relatives in North Carolina. Then, that inmate asked if I believed that he was innocent. I told him that what I believe would not make a difference and I was not in a position to make any decisions. My job, however, was to be a pastoral care provider and not a jury or a judge.

He shared how scared he used to be when the State was executing inmates. He had countless nightmares thinking that he was going to be next. He spent his adulthood incarcerated. He was hopeful that one day the truth would come to light, and he would be exonerated. The inmate prayed over and over for his freedom and still felt like his days were literally numbered and he was going to die as an innocent man. After being on death row for about thirty years, the real killer was found through Deoxyribonucleic Acid (DNA) technology, and he was set free.

There have been about four hundred people in the United States of America who have been exonerated through DNA testing, including twenty-one who served time on death row. The organization went further to state, "69% involved eyewitness misidentification, 52% involved misidentification from a photo array, 7% from a mugshot book, 54% involved an in-court misidentification, 84% of the misidentification cases involved a misidentification by a surviving victim, 29% of false confession, and 43% involved misapplication of forensic science."[21]

It is obvious that the justice system of the most prosperous and powerful country in the world is not perfect. Many people have been falsely put into prison for crimes they did not commit. Unfortunately, brown people have been disproportionately targeted and persecuted.

Throughout my tenure, I always encouraged prisoners to be pro-active instead of re-active in almost everything they do. Being pro-active means thinking about what could happen if acted a particular way. It is about playing scenarios in one's head with potential positive or negative results. In other words, I told them to try to play out, in their head, what they were about to do and look at the positive and negative sides of that action. I reminded them, that required some quick thinking, that every decision-making process has two side effects, and it is up to them to assess the risk and benefit to decide if the action was worth it. Once action is taken, one has to live with its consequences, good or bad.

Re-active, on the other hand, is the result of not having a pro-active mindset. Generally, it leads to regrets, isolation, self-disappointment, self-pity, shame, sadness, and sometimes depression.

---

[21] https://bit.ly/3qoiAUE - Access date: 7.7.2021

At the re-active stage, there is absolutely nothing one can do to change the outcome. There is always an opportunity for learning in all mistakes. Failing to learn from mistakes is a mistake. The learning process can sometimes be very emotionally painful, but the end result can be beneficial.

I learned many lessons during my transition into a maximum-security prison. The culture is different, and the environment is scary. That facility was like a small town, except, some people were free to move around whereas others were not.

Like all maximum-security prisons, sliding doors were in many locations that were monitored by a correctional officer and only that person can see that employee only after pressing a button that sends a request to open that door to let one through.

The prison system is like any other environment with its own language or jargons. Words, for instance, behind those walls could have completely different meaning than their typical use. Therefore, it is helpful to ask questions if in doubt. One day, an inmate asked a volunteer at the end of a worship service to pray for his hearing. That volunteer did not waste any time and began praying for that offender's hearing. "So, how is your hearing now?" he asked the prisoner, to which he responded, "It is next week at the courthouse."

Almost all prisons depend heavily on volunteers to organize a range of activities from worship services (for almost all religions represented) to secular functions under the supervision of paid staff. The chaplaincy's daily schedule was usually filled with several religious services and, when I was there, that prison had fifteen different religions.

Chitchats with Inmates and Volunteers

After spending one year in the death row and general population units, it was time to be transferred to two other units. It was a sad day because I had developed a healthy relationship with many of them, ministered to them, provided comfort during the death of loved ones in the free world, and listened to their stories (particularly, during their formative years).

Those men were children just like us. I am sure they had dreams to become all kinds of things in life while growing up and being charged for murder was not one of them. People do not become criminals overnight. Certain things must have happened during their upbringing and beyond. Every baby has the potential to become a good or bad citizen in this world. Environment and opportunities, in some cases, become the determining factor.

Most chaplains receive extensive academic and religious training before being able to perform their pastoral duties. They are also trained to keep their personal religious beliefs private unless asked during a pastoral conversation.

Case in point, while assigned on a death row unit, an inmate asked, "Chaplain, among all the religions in the world why did you choose Christianity to be your religion." I prefaced my answer by telling him that Christianity is a way of life and not a religion. Then, I told him that all the founding religious leaders are in the grave waiting for their judgement day except for the founder of Christianity, Jesus Christ. While he was alive, he told his followers that he was going to die, and he would be raised from the dead after three days. Voila! That is the reason I choose Christianity.

Working in a prison environment can be both rewarding and depressing. Seeing lives that are being wasted due to some poor decision-making, skin color, or simply because of lack of better parenting skills or opportunities is heart-breaking.

While I made round at a unit, I met with an inmate who was awaiting his trial. He was distraught with the idea of going before a judge even though it was his first as an adult. He told me that judge was going to add all of his previous charges when he served time as a juvenile even though it has been thirty years. After serving his time as a juvenile, his criminal record was sealed accordingly but subject to being reopened if a crime was committed as an adult. Pastoral listening was provided as he pondered over his fate as he has been a law-abiding citizen all of his adult life.

Serving time behind walls could cause inmates to lose touch with the outside world, in terms of holidays, throughout the year. As a result, we made sure we brought each holiday to the inmates by giving out cards for each occasion, for them to send out to their loved ones (if they were still in touch with them).

The most popular holiday was Mother's Day, and most of them would share some moving and emotional stories about their relationship with their mothers. Father's Day, however, was the least popular one. Weeks prior that celebration, I told them that I understood how fatherhood is an extremely sensitive topic in almost every culture.

Furthermore, I reminded them how many men tend to have a tough time getting along with their biological fathers and based on my recollection, only a handful of them requested Father's Day cards. However, I challenged those who were fathers to send the cards to their children to let them know they were thinking about them.

In the end, I urged them, to be careful about those they hate or people they cannot get along with because sometimes as we are aging we may find ourselves becoming just like them. Afterward, an inmate told me privately how he hated his father as a child because the way he used to treat him and his siblings. Then, he said that chitchat helped him to realize that he had treated his children like his father when he was in the free world.

Constantly, I reminded the offenders of two things, that my goal was to build a relationship with them, not a friendship and I was not better than them. I was very intentional when it came to treating them with respect and dignity. Losing one's freedom does not mean that person has to lose his or her dignity.

During a question-and-answer session, one inmate asked about my daily routine. I told him that I live a boring life with no exciting events. "I go to work, go grocery shopping, and care for my family" I answered. Surprisingly, he said, "Chaplain, I wish I had lived a boring life when I was in the free world because I would still be free. I am serving time now because of an exciting life."

Every now and then, I would join inmates in the prison's courtyard during their recreation time either during basketball games or tournament or just chilling out. I was intentional in spending time with them outside my office whenever I could because I wanted to build some rapport so that I could build some trust. Without a trusting relationship, impacting people's lives positively would be almost impossible.

One day, some inmates were criticizing the overall treatment they were receiving especially how poor the prison food quality was and were planning to make their discontent known formally to the facility's administration. Out of the blue, another inmate stood up and said, "Guys, do not play with your blessing because to me I feel like I am in a five-star hotel including three meals a day and the best medical treatment for free. Where I am from in the middle east some governments provide absolutely nothing to their incarcerated citizens. Inmates must rely on their families, relatives, and some kind offenders when their loved ones brought them foods or snacks."

At the end of each question-and-answer session, I always reminded inmates that I was not better than them, and a simple uncalculated decision could send me here. Also, as their chaplain I urged them never to think that God loved me more than them. God's love is unbiassed.

Whether formally through pastoral counseling in my office or during a class session in that prison's chapel, I always found a way to encourage offenders with release date to better plans for the free world if not they may keep coming back over and over. I challenged them not to be defined by their criminal record but by their full potential as humans and what they could give to our society.

I reminded them if they were not careful, they may find themselves in a deadly triangle moving from home or the street, the court system, and prisons while their lives with potential were being wasted away behind walls. Below was a graph I shared with them:

Deadly Triangle

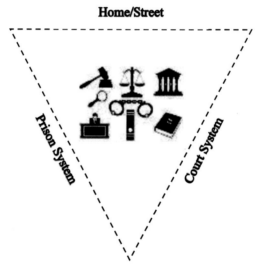

Everything starts at home or on the street where most of us if not all learn almost all of our habits and sometimes values. When things begin to become out of control from those two places, the court system must be involved because it is their job to keep peace in order to avoid chaos. Then, it is up to the court system to decide where to send those who refuse to obey local, state, and federal laws, and that is where the prison system come in.

I always concluded by reminding them it was up to them to start to unlearn some of the unacceptable habits and behaviors they had learned at home or on the street and begin to learn those acceptable ones while serving time. In other words, it must start in their mind because that is where everything starts.

One inmate, for instance, told me that his fate was decided three times in one building but different floor. The first time was as a teenager regarding guardianship, the second one was as a juvenile, and the last one when he was sentenced as a lifer.

Working in a prison is an erratic environment. Once inside, people never know how their workday will end. Whenever inmates, staff, or volunteer asked how I was doing, my answer was, "So far, so good!" A Kairos volunteer once told me, "Chaplain, you always scared me with that answer." I told him that nobody knew when this prison could turn upside down through a riot.

Kairos Prison Ministry International is a Christian faith-based ministry that addresses the spiritual needs of incarcerated men, women, youth, and their families. Based on my experience working with those volunteers and supervising them, they were professional, caring, and consistent with following a prison's policy and Standard of Operating Procedures. Most importantly, their ministry was inclusive.

During prospective and new volunteers' training, I always made sure to tell prospective volunteers that every time they, or anybody, stepped inside of any prison, there was a possibility they could go back in a body bag. Therefore, I religiously told them to never let their guard down or be comfortable around offenders because being complacent in a prison context could be one of the most dangerous attitudes employees or volunteers could have.

Also, I reminded them never to take anything from inmates to deliver someone in the free world and never bring anything to them as well in the event they know an offender's family member. As a matter of fact, they must report a social connection to a staff.

Who to Trust?

When it came to working in an adult maximum-security, each day was unpredictable. Chaplains, in most cases, had no idea where their day may start and when or where it may end. One needs to have an open mind and be willing to adjust quickly to meet offenders and employees need efficiently. They must be able to think on one's feet.

There had been times, for instance, I had my to do lists on my desk for days and never had a chance even to look at them. Sometimes, an item that was at the bottom of my list found its way to the top, simply because of an emergent need.

Upon answering my office phone, the person on the other line stated that she was calling from Child Protective Services (CPS) and would like to speak with an inmate regarding his young daughter. Her mother had been arrested and he had twenty-four hours to decide which family member would take custody of that girl or she would go in the foster care system. After asking her some key questions, I informed her that I would call her back in about an hour.

One thing, I had learned during the first months working in a maximum-security prison was to never take any information about an inmate with a *face value*. Any message could be used as a code for something. As a result, I put my investigating cap on to find out if the given information was legitimate even though that "CPS employee" had shared her credentials with me.

Many inmates tend to be highly creative with their imagination. Though serving time, they have people in the free world who are working for them to send coded messages. Therefore, almost all incoming or outgoing phone calls, that were offender related, had to be scrutinized before deciding.

For instance, I was informed of an inmate who was assigned in a Special Housing Unit (SHU) that wanted to see me because he was distraught by a letter he received to inform him of the death of his grandmother who raised him. After offering my condolences, I asked him for that letter. "I was so mad, Chaplain, I flushed it in my toilet" he replied.

Per that prison's Standard Operating Procedure (SOP) at that time, a phone call should be given to that inmate to have some emotional closure because he would not be able to attend a funeral service. Certain inmates could be escorted to a funeral home for a private viewing, only in the case of the death a family member. Within this context, only parents and siblings were considered immediate family. Grandparents and cousins, on the other hand, were considered relatives. Unless, however, there was a document to prove that his grandmother was in fact the legal guardian.

Once a death of an inmate's family member had been verified, only a clinical chaplain was allowed to give that grieving offender a phone call. Upon calling to verify the death of that offender's grandmother, to my surprise, it was the grandmother who answered the phone. She was able to confirm her information based on what we had in our system.

After telling her my reason for calling and jokingly saying, "I never thought I would talk to a dead person on the phone" we both had a laugh and she said, "Chaplain, tell my grandson he will die before me."

Afterward, I met with that inmate, and he admitted that he had lied because he wanted a phone call. During our pastoral conversation, he also confessed that he thought I was not aware of the prison's SOP in regard to phone calls.

Therefore, I was on guard when it came to the CPS story. My investigation revealed that the offender indeed did have a daughter. Upon breaking the news to him about his daughter's fate, he broke down in tears and refused to accept that information because his daughter was with his wife. He was very emotional to say the least and expressed some guilt for not being there for his little girl.

Subsequently, he became incredibly angry. In the meantime, I provided some pastoral presence, comfort, and listened to his frustration. Eventually, his anger turned into blaming his wife who was arrested for selling illegal drugs. "What was she thinking?" He rhetorically asked.

Later, he asked me what he needed to do for his daughter. I told him that CPS needed to know the name and contact of a family member that could assume legal guardianship of his daughter within twenty-four hours, otherwise they would put her into the foster care system.

"Do you have the information that CPS requested?" I inquired. "No," he replied. He said, "Chaplain, many of my relatives are either drug dealers or addicted to drugs. I will never let my daughter near the other half of my family due to their sexual immoralities." Then, he asked, "What do you think I should do, sir?"

After challenging him to ponder over the situation and scrutinize his circle, inner circle, and mini circle to find someone, he came up with nobody. I told him that the only thing I could do was to ask the CPS agent for an extra day or two to give his decision. In conclusion, that offender could not find a trusted family member or a friend to become his daughter's legal guardian while he and his wife were serving time in the North Carolina adult prisons.

I dealt with several cases like that one during my five-year-tenure as a clinical chaplain. Based on my experience, unfortunately, a handful of inmates were able to find someone in their entourage who could be trusted in case of an emergency with their children.

Chapter Fifteen

Ex-Offenders' Company, Re-Entry Program, and Hospitalization

During my tenure as a clinical chaplain, I was intentional with my pastoral care approach. I always found ways to spend time and fellowship with them either behind or outside of the penitentiary walls.

Most humans learn through socialization and not isolation. It is through healthy relationships that new and acceptable social manners can be learned or adapted. The opposite is also true for non-acceptable social behaviors.

While working with the juveniles, I used weekly good behaviors as an incentive to take them to social activities in neighboring communities either religious gatherings, volunteering, or attending a game in an arena. We also had a Friday gathering and only those with no write up for the week could attend where they ate pizza, drank soft drinks, and at the end had a movie night with popcorn.

Those juveniles thoroughly enjoyed those moments, to say the least. There was a tremendous change in behaviors with that positive reinforcement approach. Humans like to be reminded that they are doing well and their efforts in improving themselves have been noticed and applauded.

Hiring With One Condition

After about a year in the adult prison system, I was invited to a quarterly meeting and lunch with mostly ex-offenders and volunteers. One of many goals was to continue providing moral, social, and spiritual support as they were re-integrating into the mainstream society and especially the workforce.

All of them shared how impossible it was to find a job upon release from prison. Unfortunately, most of them have children and being a provider like a good father should was a challenge. Many of them tempted to go back to their previous life of selling drugs, but they also realized that they were too old for the prison game.

It could be very discouraging and frustrating, after serving time for a crime committed, when persons have no way of supporting themselves and their family simply because of a background check. Let me be clear, I am not against conducting background checks because there some people with ill intentions in our society. An effective proactive re-entry system, nevertheless, should be in place to ease those who are doing their best to follow the law and stay on the narrow road.

As offenders are having tough times finding work due to their criminal record, some North Carolina inmates have taken matters into their own hands and become creative by starting their own company. In the job application, nevertheless, once applicants responded negatively when asked if they had been arrested before, they shredded that application. Their goal is to hire ex-offenders only.

It was during those meetings that I came to realize how challenging and impossible it was for someone with a criminal record to be hired for any type of employment. Is it fair for someone to be treated still like an outcast in our society after serving time in a penitentiary?

Re-Entry Program

America appears to have an informal caste system like India within their justice system. Almost nobody wants to be associated with someone with a criminal record. I think that could be one of many reasons the rate of recidivism is so prevalent. There seems to be no second chances in that system unless those ex-offenders have excellent financial family support where they will find jobs with no background check conducted.

Criminal law can be amended to allow an ex-convict to find jobs and become contributing members of our society. Unless, some laws are amended in this country, juvenile and adult facilities will always be a place for wasting human potential.

"The United States has some of the highest recidivism rates in the world. According to the National Institute of Justice, almost 44% of criminals released return before the first year out of prison. In 2005, about 68% of 405,000 released prisoners were arrested for a new crime within three years, and 77% were arrested within five years."[22]

Without a less judgmental re-entry program, it would be almost impossible for the recidivism rate to go down. Lawmakers cannot talk about their desire to fight crimes without addressing the elephant released offenders face when attempting to apply for a job. Unless prison discrimination is effectively addressed, crime rates will always be skyrocketing. The US justice system seems to focus more on punishment than rehabilitation. The latter one places emphasis on the person rather than his or her crimes.

Due to a poor re-entry program, the justice system, inadvertently, creates frequent fliers into the prison facilities. These individuals often cycle among jails and prisons, halfway houses, hospital emergency rooms, to the streets, and the cycle continues.

The Netherlands have become a model when it comes to criminal justice system. "Between 2009 and 2018, the Dutch justice system has closed a total of thirty-one prisons because the crime rate plummeted to the lowest level since 1980. The reason attributed to the decrease in crimes includes shorter sentencing for crimes related to drugs and substance abuse and imposing stricter

---

[22] https://bit.ly/38SKnaA- Access date: June 15, 2021

fines rather than incarceration. These prisons have been converted into refugee centers, housing, and hotels."[23]

Hospitalization

During my tenure at that maximum-security prison, I saw many frequent fliers. Some of them were candid about their reason for their return into the prison system by acknowledging the fact that they could not find work, eat, and a place to sleep. They concluded that the only way to find free food, free housing, and have the best healthcare accessible was to commit another crime.

For instance, during my hospital rounds, I was surprised to see an inmate who was released about nine months prior. Before his release, we met every two weeks to prepare him to understand that the world he left years ago was a completely different society in terms of technology and lifestyle.

Without asking about his reason for being back, he told me that four months after his release he was diagnosed with cancer. "Chap, (a short way of saying the word chaplain) with no health insurance, committing another crime was the only way to receive the best medical care," he concluded. I wished him all the best as he was fighting cancer.

When I was assigned to the prison hospital, I had the privilege to be present, provide companionship, and spiritually support inmates who were dealing with all kinds of illnesses. It was one thing to be incarcerated and it was heartbreaking to be hospitalized where loved ones could not visit to provide emotional support.

If and when surgeries were needed, those ill inmates were transported to a local hospital with at least two correctional officers

---

[23] https://bit.ly/3qfT8Bw - Access date: 6.15.2021

in the room 24/7 even in the operating room. Per that prison's SOP, those inmates' legs ought to be shackled as well as one hand handcuffed to the steel of their hospital bed even throughout the dying process.

Unfortunately, hospitalized offenders' families were not allowed to visit except when death was imminent. With my supervisor's blessing, I was allowed to visit some of them once a month while they were being treated in some local hospitals. I felt morally obligated as their pastor to continue supporting them, spiritually, inside their prison and hospital walls.

One particular inmate was dying with cancer and his loved ones lived in a different state. He could only communicate with them via letters. Unfortunately, there was no accessible phones in the hospital for offenders to use at that time. It was a critical and sad situation.

In my line of work, chaplains sometimes must become advocates and be the voice to the voiceless. After meeting with the hospital's chief executive officer (CEO), he allowed me to use a wireless phone from his office and grant that offender a ten-to-twenty-minute weekly phone call to his wife and daughter until he could no longer talk. He and family were extremely grateful.

During his dying journey, I assisted him in reviewing his life with his family especially his daughter as he was not active in her life. After all, he was able to mail them a package to express regrets and asked them for forgiveness for he had failed them. In his daughter's package, he sent a list of things he wished he had taught her as a father.

Mental Health

Based on my experience with the justice system, as well as reviewing much published research, I have found that all jails and prisons have inmates who are suffering with mental illness.

Case in point, according to Stanford Law School, *Three Strikes Project*, "Mentally ill inmates represent 45% of the total California prison population, and 55% are non-mentally ill " These statistics might be true in all facilities across the United States of America as the prison population grows daily and many of them have some forms of mental issues.

The research continues and alludes, "The cascade, which began so long ago, has created a new segregation—the segregation of the sick, the infirm and the helpless (many of whom are also people of color, almost all of whom are extremely poor). Not unlike other practices of segregation in our nation's history, this segregation is also hidden from the general public behind the walls of our prisons and jails. But this time it is not occurring in the form of slavery on individual farms and homes – today it is occurring behind the bars of prison cells."[24]

When I was assigned to the mental health unit, I was exposed to people dealing with mental illnesses for the first time. Many of them were not allowed to be around other inmates even during socialization in their shared area due to their mental illness severity. Providing spiritual care support was extremely challenging for many of them because they were in a completely differently world. For my safety's sake, I was only allowed to minister to them through their door, individually. Even those with mild mental illness, required one or two correctional officers be nearby because of their behavioral unpredictability.

---

[24] https://stanford.io/3KTUtWz - Access date:10.2.2021

After receiving an urgent pastoral visit request from one of them, I considered it a priority to visit him before my shift ended. He thanked me for coming on a short notice. He wanted me to contact the Federal Bureau of Investigation (FBI) regarding a credible plot he had received that someone was going to assassinate President Barack Obama. "I cannot tell you the source of my information, Chaplain," he replied after asking him. I told him that it was imperative to give me the source of that threat because the FBI would ask me that same question.

Consequently, as soon as I began sharing that with the sergeant on duty, he knew exactly who had sent me that request because he had received that same message countless times. We both laughed about the situation.

Looking back on my tenure with that prison, I concluded that the mental health unit was the most challenging one because I never had the chance to provide one-on-one pastoral care support or assist them to review and process certain areas in their lives. Unfortunately, many of them never graduated to the general population unit.

In the event of the death of a family member, after allowing them a phone call to speak with a loved one, they did not have the mental capacity to process that loss. Prior to informing mental health inmates of a family death, I had to speak with their psychiatrist and psychologist to know whether or not that offender would understand. As a result, some relatives would become upset with me when I told them that the moment was not appropriate to inform that person per his mental health team care.

My most memorable moment was witnessing their mental progress and being prepared by attending some behavioral classes before sending them to the general population. Many of them, however, for whatever reason, would go back to the mental health unit within days or weeks.

In recent years, the prison system has seen in increase in their mental health illness population. As a result, it seems that jails and penitentiaries are becoming the new mental health facility.

Chapter Sixteen

Religions and Gangsterism, Preaching and Lawsuit, and Freedom

In most cases, it seems that only through adversities can life's lessons be learned, and any religious faith be tested. For some, unfortunately, those lessons are being learned behind concrete walls. Within this context, there are those who use religion as a coping mechanism or a way to kill time by finding religious activities to keep themselves occupied while serving time.

During my tenure at that maximum-security prison as a clinical chaplain, I had the privilege to baptize many inmates by immersion upon formal request. During those years performing believer's baptism, only one offender declined to take the eight-week class I recommended. He told me that he had no time to waste sitting in a class. I wanted to ask him if he was scheduled to go somewhere because as an inmate time was all he had, but instead I wished him all the best.

Teaching a baptismal class is important because it helps candidates to have a sound doctrinal understanding before entering or engaging into any religious ritual. The Christian Bible is silent about baptismal catechism, but it is an opportunity to learn.

One of many things I told them was if they wanted to be baptized with the intent to be saved, they would be wasting their time because water baptism does not save and that is the reason it is called believer's baptism. In other words, the belief must come prior to the immersion.

Listening to their conversion stories was important in the process because they helped me in understanding their spiritual journey better. One baptismal candidate, for instance, grew up in India. He shared how confusing it was as a boy, learning about a myriad of gods and did not know which one was right or correct. There was a god for almost everything. As he began studying other religions, he started developing a deep and sincere interest in

Christianity as a monotheistic religion. As a result, his parents threatened to abandon him if he was to leave Hinduism.

For many, religions in the prison system can be considered as a means of survival. As a result, some people including inmates tend to be skeptical about inmates' religious beliefs and expressions of faith. For instance, Jarvis Masters, a death row inmate in San Quentin, California, in one of his books, *Finding Freedom,* asserted that he has been incarcerated most of his life and he does not trust any inmate when it comes religion.

My job was to pastor them and not to assess or question their relationship with a higher being. It was, however, to facilitate and accommodate whenever possible to meet their spiritual needs as it is crucial for any individual, free or in captivity, to seek a sacred connection.

Believe it or not, the term religious freedom also exists in the prison system. As a trained Christian chaplain, I never asked offenders for reasons when they requested to change their religion. I thought that was personal.

One day, however, I was shocked and disappointed after receiving a religious change form from an inmate whom I had baptized two weeks earlier. Based on my numerous encounters with him, he seemed to be sincere in his walk with God.

Within twenty-four hours after changing his religion to Judaism, he was apologetic about his decision when he entered my office. I told him that there was no need to apologize because it was his decision and I respected it. He went on to say that Jewish meals are healthier than the general population ones and realized that the best way to eat healthy was to be become Jewish. After listening to him, I reminded him that he did not owe me any explanation.

Some offenders would change their religion months in advance for an upcoming religious feast, which at that time allowed outside food to come into the prison from an approved vendor. Based on my observation, Islam seemed to be the most popular one because of Ramadan where a colossal feast was usually held at the end of the month of fasting.

The next most popular one was the Native American religion where state issued tobacco was used to send prayers through pipe smoking. A small portion of state government approved tobacco was given to all those assigned to that particular religion, and that worship service was held outside.

However, if it rained or snowed, all outside activities were cancelled and their religious service was held inside where they could watch a movie about their religion, or an adherent would read some chapters from a Native American book. Strangely enough, those indoor religious services were usually attended by one third or less.

During my tenure, I heard inmates refer to the Native American religion as a smoking club. Countless Native American adherents had been caught attempting to smuggle their state issued tobacco inside to sell to heavy smokers or to trade for snacks. If caught, the offender would spend at least three weeks in solitary confinement.

There were those who joined a particular religion for protection, especially if that particular religious group had some well-respected gang members. Feeling safe and protected was and still is the nature of any prison from a juvenile facility to a maximum-security one.

As a chaplain with a Christian faith background, I had the privilege of teaching several classes, *History of the Christian Bible, History of Baptism, Basic Understanding of the Christian Faith,* upon request by the Christian inmate community. After the completion of those three months, all participants received a certificate.

The Politics of Gangs

Gangsterism seems to play an integral role in the life of any prison. Most inmates, especially young ones, will follow someone and that leader in return could provide some kind of protection. They seem to be well organized and communicate through different means. For instance, they used hand gestures like the hearing-impaired use as a communicating tool.

Religious services and gangsterism to some extent go hand and hand because that is where gang members deliver messages to other inmates, especially during prayer time or during dismissal as they leave their chapel. Most inmates can be highly creative in finding ways to further their gang activities behind those concrete walls even during religious services or any social gathering.

I was ignorant when it came to knowing gangs' signs and their meanings because no formal training was provided to chaplains. Therefore, I used to watch correctional officers on alert during religious services for any messages that were being sent or any transfer of contraband among inmates.

Those who mastered the gangsterism means of communication had to keep sharpening that skill and attending continuing education because offenders kept altering signs to avoid being understood. It seemed an endless game of cat and mouse among offenders and correctional officers.

Prisons at all levels of security are dominated by gang members. They have their own way of communicating by using their hands and body languages to send sensitive and critical messages to their members. That is why non-certified correctional employees must rely on certified correctional officers, with proper training, during any type of gathering. It is believed that religious services are usually used as meeting places to pass on gang info.

"Power in the Blood!" That was the title of a message a volunteer wrote on a white board in the prison's chapel before he started a Christian Bible study. He began by stating the importance of being under the blood and its protection (He was referring to the blood of Jesus Christ).

"Chaplain, can I talk to you right away, please?" a correctional sergeant requested. We left the chapel quietly and went into an office while the assigned correctional officer remained behind to continue providing security. I could see the seriousness on his face as he asked, "Is the volunteer recruiting inmates to join the blood gangsters?" "What!" I exclaimed. "What do you mean?" I asked. "Well, his title on the white board was power in the blood." I told him I did not think so, but he was more than welcome to stay and observe how the volunteer was going to develop his topic. At the end the worship service, we all had a big laugh about the context in which the title was used, could be misunderstood, and how a completely different message could be sent or interpreted.

After supervising a religious service on death row, I had the opportunity to chat with an inmate and he told me that death row saved his life. "Sir, you know you are here to be executed, what do you mean by 'death row saved your life?'" I asked him to explain his own oxymoron.

He took a deep breath and said, "When I was in the free world, I lived an extremely destructive life. I was involved in many criminal activities, I hurt and killed people in the process. Frankly, I thought I was invincible. Chaplain, I believe if I were still out there, I would have been dead because of rival gangs. I have been on death row for the past twenty years."

Gangsterism in Haiti

It would be hypocritical of me to talk about religion and gangsterism without mentioning its negative and damaging impact in my country. Since the introduction of democracy in my homeland by the US government in 1986, there has been a political vacuum. This has led to one crisis after another.

As a result, there has been almost no political stability with zero long-term governmental strategic plans. Most politicians are becoming richer while the rest of the population who chose them are barely surviving. Being involved in politics has become a self-centered career versus a people centered one. They should be called "pollical mercenaries" instead of politicians because they seem to be money driven above everything else.

From 1986 to now, Haitian people have been living in chronic instability and its negative impact is enormous and seems to be worsening daily. Unfortunately, since the introduction of so called "democracy" in the island, it has been producing mostly political mercenaries. The new way of governance introduced by the US was over-promised and under-delivered. People cannot introduce democracy without tackling illiteracy in a nation where it is about 80%. It is no doubt a formula for chaos because democracy goes hand in hand with formal education. No one can talk about a democratic nation while most of its citizens cannot read and write.

As a result, every aspect of Haitian society has been negatively affected by this national crisis, the political instability, and insecurity. I tend to compare my country of birth as a person with a metastatic tumor. Fortunately, those tumors are not malignant. They are treatable with proactive leadership, social, political, and religious togetherness with intentional aggressive treatments. Bear in mind that this process might take decades to see positive results.

Hence, it will require a national consciousness to work in unison for a common goal to leave a better quality of life for generations to come. Unfortunately, there seems to be a group of individuals who profit from its current alarming and heart-breaking conditions.

Without that mindset of proactivity, there will be no concrete hope for young Haitians with dreams of a better tomorrow. People without hope are the most fragile and dangerous ones in any society. Consequently, that could result in all kinds of criminal enterprises such as gangsterism and kidnaping just to name these two most popular ones.

One of the key players in any society is the church with a social and spiritual mission to change people's lives positively. Churches should promote hope and create opportunities to improve lives and if time permits preach later. Preaching about hell and heaven only will not make people's lives better while on earth. In fact, it may create resentment toward God because of our failed mission as church leaders.

Heaven and people's souls are crucial for the afterlife but what about life on earth? Oliver Wendell Holmes Sr., an American medical doctor and poet was right when he said, "Some people are so heavenly minded that they are no earthly good."[25] You cannot have heaven in mind while neglecting God's children on earth.

The fundamental message of God whom we claim to be His representatives is based on love and not division. But Protestantism in Haiti seems so divided that each denomination is treated as a rival or competitor while God's people are perishing. If we claim that we are worshiping the same God, we should then strive to work together for a better nation under God.

Due to political instability and no proper government that can bring about law and order, gangsters and kidnapers seem to be everywhere, and people's daily lives are crippled. Sadly, gangsters and kidnapers seem more unified and organized than local governments and religious groups.

Gangsterism in most cases is the result of socioeconomic inequality. It is a complex phenomenon, but its roots seem to come from broken families and lack of social opportunities for those in the lower-class echelon.

---

[25] https://bit.ly/36b6FDh - Access date: 1.20.2022

Based on my professional experience as a clinical chaplain in a juvenile and death row prison, gang members usually feel ignored and marginalized by the mainstream society; therefore, they look for a sense of belonging and breadwinning in an unorthodox fashion in order to survive and feed their families through organized criminal activities that may involve threat and violence in most cases.

During a most recent interview with an amateur reporter, one of the gangs' leaders said that they were willing to lay down their weapons if they could find work to feed their families. One of them went on to say that as a young man he could not watch his children dying of hunger while staying idle. He added that desperate situations required desperate measures.

The informal enterprise has not only affected the national life, but it has also destroyed the tourism industry. Tourists would like to feel safe when traveling and visiting historical sites. Only local and federal governments can create that safe environment and these two have been almost non-existent since 1986.

Case in point, Haitians regardless of their socio-economic backgrounds, kidnap on a regular basis and families have to find ways to pay for their loved ones' release. In October 2021, gang members kidnapped a group of seventeen Canadian and US missionaries (including an eight-month-old baby), and they demanded a ransom of 17 million US dollars. Fortunately, they were released after spending two months in captivity and there have been conflicting news reports whether or not a ransom was paid.

In the midst of this national crisis, the police appears to have become powerless. It has been reported that due to insecurity, police stations were abandoned. Before judging the police force, bear in mind that there were formerly about ten thousand soldiers and military police officers on the island. But the United States Marines, *Operation Uphold Democracy,* invaded Haiti in September 1994 under the 42nd president, William Jefferson Clinton. The

Haitian army disbanded, the exiled president Jean-Bertrand Aristide returned, and a police force was started.

Based on multiple videos circulating on social media, those gangsters and kidnappers may have more powerful and sophisticated weapons than the national police force and other special forces. The biggest piece of that puzzle has been and still is how did they find those weapons? Are there powerful people behind those organized crimes? Is it fair to say that there has been a security vacuum since the US government dissolved the national army? Consequently, gangsterism has been in the making to fill that void. What happen to those ransoms that those kidnappers have been collecting?

What should be done to that metastatic tumor that is destroying the once called, *Pearl of the Caribbean*? It will require a national effort. Most importantly, all religious leaders regardless of their understanding of a higher power should come together for the common good of the Haitian people to stop the spread of that virus.

Sadly, evangelism and preaching about heaven and hell will not cure it. In fact, it might make it worse because even religious leaders recently have been affected negatively by the spread of that tumor. They have been kidnapped, injured, or killed during religious services. Those living or should I say surviving in ghettos do not need to be evangelized right now. They need to be loved and cared for.

Regrettably, some religious leaders seem to focus more on building their own kingdom on earth instead of God's while ignoring the marginalized people. They, too, are "ministerial mercenaries" because their primary focus seem to be money and not people's wellbeing. Building congregational schools has been a dividing tool among citizens in terms of pride and superiority. They have built them with a camouflaged intent to "help" the poor, but their tuitions are higher than their counterparts.

Those people need love in action and to be evangelized later. It is crucial to zero in on first things first, that is, people's wellbeing before anything else. They need your compassion in a such a way to help them develop a certain level of independence while enhancing their dignity without putting them down. People's basic needs are more important than political discourses and religious sermons.

For instance, they need fulltime employment so that they can feed their families and forge a better future for themselves and their progenitors. They need money to feed their children and send them to school so that their future can be better than their parents.

It has been reported by a news outlet that kidnappers use their ransom money to feed families in their neighborhoods, pay school tuitions for students, and cover medical and prescriptions expenses for those who cannot afford them especially the aged.

They need better living conditions like everyone else. Regrettably, local and federal governments are unable to create social stability in order for investors to open businesses. It is time for religious leaders to start using God's money they have been collecting weekly, and sometimes two to three times a week, and begin investing in God's people and not buildings. Human beings are more important than programs, constructions, and edifices. Saving money in banks while the unfortunate ones are in desperate need of social and financial help is not love.

People are the center of politics and ministry; therefore, politicians and religious leaders should go back to their basic mission that is to serve people and not the other way around. It is time for those two sectors to be people focused and not self-centered.

As I stated earlier, Haiti's tumors have been metastasized, but they are not cancerous. All religious leaders regardless of their theological beliefs, understanding, and faith traditions should begin working together with a common goal to improve the lives of God's people because all religions believe in helping the needy. For those of you who are Christians, remember that you all are

God's hands and feet while on earth. It is time to show your faith in action.

Without that general consensus and effort, people's suffering will be worsened. It is time for all sectors to live up to the national coat of arms of Haiti, *L' Union fait la Force, Unity is Strength.* Division or rivalry will not help us move forward. Our ancestors were united in fighting for their independence. Now, it is our turn to do likewise to save our homeland through organized programs that would improve the lives of the now generation and ones to come.

Remember, the international community cannot do it for us even though there are those who believe they can. Neighbors cannot keep coming to clean up your mess. They, too, have their own cleaning to do in their house. It is our responsibility to build our nation like they are doing for theirs. We cannot spend the rest of our lives depending on other nations. Unfortunately, another group has been fasting and praying for a divine intervention without playing their part. Throughout the history of humanity, God has been and still is in the business of using people to carry out His will.

Case in point, if we were waiting for the international community to free us from slavery, we would still be in bondage. Other countries have their own problems to deal with. They can only supply a helping hand in order for us to stand and work hard on our own and improve our lives.

Political and religious leaders have national and international connections and resources. Therefore, it is time to start putting them together for the betterment of your people. There is a great need for reformation within those mentioned sectors because they are filled with mercenaries, which hopefully will lead to a social and moral consciousness.

Instead of pointing fingers while the poor are going deeper into poverty, it is time to put sociopolitical, ideological, theological, and doctrinal differences aside, meet, and brainstorm ideas on how to invest in the most vulnerable communities. The time is now to conduct local surveys to find out what products the population use the most and are not readily available and produce them. Pull your national and international connections and resources together to build factories in or near ghettos for citizens and gang members to find jobs to support themselves and their loved ones.

Create social empowerment programs through jobs training and build professional schools where young people can learn trade. Stop pretending to be helping the poor while hurting them instead by living luxurious lifestyles while they are dying in poverty. Start working together and plan a proactive social revolution with central basic needs in mind because we are running out of time.

Lao Tzu, an ancient Chinese philosopher and writer, was on point when he said that if you give a hungry man a fish, you feed him for a day, but if you teach him how to fish, you feed him for a lifetime.[26] The time is now for political and religious leaders to start teaching people how to fish by creating and supplying opportunities for them.

Remember, leadership is about serving the people and not the contrary. The gangsterism phenomenon in any society is the result of family dynamics and social disparity!

---

[26] https://bit.ly/36gGDOR - Access date: 1.20.2022

Preaching and Lawsuit

The prison system is an extension of our society where one finds people from all walks of life and a sample of all professions one could think of are serving time. As a chaplain, I had the privilege to develop a healthy pastoral relationship with all of them and not a friendship. After all, I am paid to be their pastor and minister to their religious and spiritual needs.

The chaplaincy department at that maximum-security prison was well structured. We had a large active volunteer program. Most religious services were led by those volunteers and chaplains supervised.

I was blessed to join the chaplaincy team when chaplains were not required to preach on Sundays during the Christian worship services for general population and death row inmates at various times.

Frankly, it would have been too much for a clergy with young children to be working five days a week, being on-call rotation during the week after working hours in the event an offender died and preparing sermons for Sunday's religious services.

Additionally, per that prison's SOP, only chaplains could inform the death of an inmate to his family. Some loved ones were not happy when we called them in the middle of the night. I was not happy either when I received those phone calls from the prison but that was what I signed up for. It was a struggle trying to fall asleep again afterward.

Anyway, when it came to requesting to have a pastoral meeting, offenders had to make a formal request. However, emergencies were dealt with on a case-by-case basis because many of them were highly creative in fabricating emergencies.

"How can I help you?" I asked an inmate who had sent a request. "Chaplain, before I filed a lawsuit based on a religious discrimination against the chaplaincy department, I would like to give you the opportunity to amend things," he stated. He continued by saying that he was a local pastor prior coming here and would like to continue his ministry through preaching and teaching in chapel while serving his time. In case you wondered about my credentials, I had a master's degree in theology.

I thanked him for his desire and willingness to serve and told him that I would like to ask him a question before we continued. "What would you do if you went to the infirmary and to your surprise a fellow inmate with his stethoscope was ready to check your heartbeat and to give you some pills for your malaise?" was my question. He exclaimed, "Oh, hell no! "I would never let another inmate be my doctor." Then, I looked at him and smiled, "Did you know that some of your fellow offenders were physicians before coming here?" "Oh, I see!" He stated. He continued to say, "What you are trying to tell me, chaplain, is that here I am an inmate and not a pastor." I told him that if that were his understanding, I would accept it. That was the end of that potential lawsuit.

Some inmates would use the term "religious freedom" and try to come up with any religious requirement in the name of their chosen religion. Having a working knowledge of all the fifteen religions in that prison was crucial as well as the religious policy. Having said that, one of my colleagues used to say that religious policy was like a sacred book in the prison system, which should be used regularly.

Freedom

Being a chaplain for two units in that prison was time consuming and demanding. Meeting offenders' spiritual needs, however, was rewarding especially when assisting them in some soul searching before their scheduled release date within six months or so. My goal was to prepare them for the world they had left years ago.

I used to remind them that they should learn to take care of their freedom upon release. Being able to move around in the free world came with responsibility, and that is the reason there are laws we must follow in order to keep enjoying that freedom; otherwise, it would be taken away.

I also challenged them to be proactive in everything they would do by encouraging them to start learning to think before speaking or doing anything. It would take some practice, but it would be worth it. For instance, I told them upon their release any encounter with law enforcement for a minor infraction such as failure to stop completely at a stop sign could lead them back into the prison system. On the other hand, someone with no criminal record may only receive a warning.

During a group session, one particular inmate told me not to worry about him because he had his release plan under control. He intended to migrate to a different state to start a new life because he wanted to stay away from drugs and some bad people in his hometown in North Carolina. I told him that a change of location was not the solution because there would be drugs and bad people wherever he went. In other words, if one's heart has not changed, a change of location would not alter behaviors. Any long and lasting change should start within and not with the outer.

I am convinced that internal change tends to have greater impact on people's behaviors more than anything else. Unfortunately, many people seem to minor on the inward and major on the outward part. It is typically about appearance.

About one year after his release, sadly, I was informed that he and one of his friends were killed during a home invasion looking for money to buy drugs in that state he had migrated to. He was also one those inmates I baptized during my tenure.

234

Chapter Seventeen
Prison Break, Death, Pastoral Support, and Time to Leave

Thursday, October 12, 2017, was a typical workday. I left the prison at about 7:30 PM after supervising a Christian Bible study for the prison general population. On my way to the lobby, I was informed by someone from the upcoming shift that there was a prison break at Pasquotank Correctional Institution (PCI), Elizabeth City, NC.

Two employees were murdered, and some gravely injured during the breakout. Those escapees did not make it far thanks to some staff and local law enforcement's swift response. In the meantime, the city was on high alert. As a result, schools and businesses were closed and citizens were encouraged to stay indoors until further notice.

I vaguely mentioned it to my wife that night because I did not know any details. The next morning, I was summoned to travel to PCI to provide pastoral care. I only had the chance to pack some clothes and kissed my family to say goodbye.

North Carolina Department of Public Safety is a big family and when a member hurts, everyone feels it. As I was making some last minutes preparation before departing for my mission, the atmosphere throughout that prison was sad. One could feel the grief.

Sent on a Mission

After saying goodbye to my supervisor and colleagues, it was time to hit the road with a fellow chaplain. I asked God for guidance and wisdom throughout that trip because I was confused and nervous. It was my first experience going to a prison where some of my colleagues were victims of a violent crime during an attempted prison break.

Candidly, I did not know what to expect, and how I was supposed to provide pastoral support in that unprecedented circumstance. Nevertheless, I was ready to go and hopeful I could make a positive impact in the lives of those survivors, grieving families, colleagues, and inmates (if allowed).

Before we finally arrived at that prison, we went through multiple check points where local law enforcement and correctional officers checked our identification cards. We reported to the command center and were briefed about what happened and we were given our assignments for the next few days.

Other chaplains were also called, and they had to travel three-to-five hours one way to go to Elizabeth City because all the neighboring correctional medium facilities had no chaplains on staff due to a state budget cut several years prior.

Even those prisons that had chaplains did not have enough. Case in point, that same prison only had two chaplains for over nine hundred inmates, and not including employees. Frankly, it was humanly impossible to provide effective pastoral care in such context.

Pastoral Care during Tragedy

Anyway, the next morning some chaplains were dispatched to some local hospitals and my team to various homes. Before leaving, one of the state leaders and I visited the crime scene. Forty-eight hours later, I could still smell fresh blood from the floor and retraced those criminals attempted escape route. It was concluded that those involved had mastered every single staff's daily routine and looked for loopholes.

I had the privilege to meet with many victims' loved ones and colleagues. I spent countless hours with them, listened to their stories and survivors' guilt while providing pastoral presence, companionship, and comfort in the midst of their sudden grief and emotional turmoil.

Unfortunately, my team was not allowed to visit the inmate population. However, days later the restriction was lifted and other teams who came later were able to provide some pastoral support to them. I was glad to hear that because, in most cases, prisoners tend to be neglected spiritually after such cruel acts. Regardless, in a situation, everybody needs to be listened to because pastoral listening can be a powerful tool during any crisis

Days later, the warden of that prison resigned upon request. It seems to be customary for wardens to step down whether or not a prison break is successful. While providing support to his staff, most of them spoke highly of him as a good leader who would find time to listen to them.

During my mission, I was impressed by the southern hospitality some local businesses and citizens exhibited by bringing meals each day. Others sent or brought flowers and thinking of you balloons or cards. It felt like almost the whole community wanted to provide support one way or another.

Crisis can sometimes bring people together for a common cause. Humanity was alive and in action during those challenging moments in that small town with a population of less than eighteen thousand.

At the end of my mission, I was asked to stay longer, which I declined because I missed my family so much and I felt emotionally drained. Even though there were great emotional needs at that prison and different homes, I knew it was time to leave.

On my way back home, my colleague and I met my supervisor and another chaplain half-way as they, too, were summoned to report to that prison. We briefed them about the situation on the ground and wished them all the best.

After reflecting and pondering over the crime scene, stories of survivors, parents who left children behind, those employees' moral, mental, and emotional state. I realized that it did not take long for some of those people's lives to change forever.

Generally, people's futures are unpredictable. We will never know when our lives will turn upside down. Those who lost their lives as well as the ones who became paralyzed probably had plans. Several of those survivors were weeks away from retiring.

Professionally, it was a life changing experience. It was the first time I dealt with so much grief and so many raw emotions in a brief period of time. Upon returning to work, I briefed some of the administration chain of command (as my direct supervisor was absent).

When I relayed the understaffing concern, I was told that there were jobs posted on the internet and nobody applied, and it could be because the prison was kind of in the middle of nowhere. I told them if the state salary offer was competitive like its counterpart, some people would even migrate to that small city.

Based on my informal investigation, many state employees were also receiving government assistance. There were those who also worked on their days off to make ends meet. Unless, the salary system changed, state employees were paid monthly. However, I used to tell people that that we were paid *weakly* compared to our counterparts, federal staff.

Anyway, about two weeks later, I penned a five-page report of my mission with some recommendations and sent it to the NC prison leadership and lawmakers. In that report, I inquired about the inmate versus correctional officers' ratio in NC because that was a red flag during the prison break where that facility was understaffed for a long time. I received no acknowledgement of that package from any leader.

Time to Leave Death Row Prison

Consequently, I began showing concern for my personal safety when supervising religious services in regard to the number of inmates versus officers providing security. I asked that same question two years prior to the prison break during a meeting with a high-ranking administrator and he said, "I don't know the answer to that and will get back to you." By the way, he never did until he retired.

Some prisons' break attempts and other violent acts toward staff, in recent years, began to preoccupy my mind and as a result I started feeling that my time with the adult prison system seemed to be coming to an end. In most cases, any prison break attempt could lead to loss of lives. Most inmates would do whatever it took, including killing someone in the process to go back to the free world they did not seem to appreciate.

Years ago, assaults used to be among inmates. Unfortunately, the pendulum shifted and that concerned me because, after all, those offenders had nothing to lose. Assaulting staff would only result in sending them to a hole for twenty-three hours with one-hour recreation periods for weeks. In the worst case (if death occurred), the state attorney general could make a case for death penalty and that would be a lengthy process with appeals in the court system.

While working full time with the juvenile justice system, I also worked two weekends a month as a Pro Re Nata (PRN) spiritual care counselor with Hospice of Wake County and now Transitions LifeCare (TL).

I felt drawn to hospice care early in my chaplaincy career because it was a great avenue to provide pastoral support to patients and loved ones who were going through some of life's challenging and emotional moments.

Prisons and hospitals have been and still are two of my preferred peculiar ministerial venues. In Matthew 25:36b, Jesus said,

"…I was sick, and you visited me, I was in prison, and you came to me."[27] Generally, those places are characterized by individuals dealing with crisis and they are usually in great distress.

Nobody deserves to go to a moment of crisis alone. Most of us may forget who came to our birthday celebrations but we will never forget those who support us in our moments of needs and challenges.

A year after that tragic prison break, I resigned from the adult prison system after almost eight years of service to accept a full-time Float Spiritual Care Counselor position with Transitions LifeCare. It was not an easy decision. After pondering and praying about it, my wife and I felt it was time to begin a new chapter. That was one of my best professional decisions to join the Transitions Lifecare organization.

One week after submitting my resignation, my supervisor and the chaplaincy team wanted to organize a farewell party for my five years of public service with the North Carolina Department of Public Safety division of adult prison. I thanked them for thinking about me and told them that I would like to leave the same way I came here, quietly. Consequently, we all had breakfast together and they wished me well in my upcoming professional chapter. It was an honor to have been part of an excellent chaplaincy team within NCDPS.

Frankly, I did not want any inmates to know about my departure even though I considered that I had a healthy pastoral relationship with the inmate's community. Nevertheless, I still wanted my departure to be a low key one. My last ministerial act was to baptize some inmates in the prison's chapel the last Sunday of October 2018. In my remarks, I urged them not to let prison determine their entire life, but instead to use that stop as a learning curve.

---

[27] NIV

About one month later, while taking my oldest son to school, who was seven years old, he said, "Daddy, I am glad you are no longer in prison." What do you mean? I inquired. Knowing him, he had a reason for making that statement.

"When you were working in the prison, you only took me school two days in a week. Also, I never saw you in the morning because when I woke up you already left for work. Sometimes, I would be in bed when you came home from work. Now, we eat breakfast and dinner together," he explained. That experience taught me that my presence was missed greatly.

After serving North Carolinians through a juvenile and adult facility as a chaplain, I had come to some conclusions that criminal activities can be learned and unlearned. The latter one, however, would take time, energy, and proactive tactical approaches with the intent to rehabilitate into society and not to punish. Punishments tend to have short term remedy whereas teaching and rehabilitation have positive and long-term benefits.

Human beings are products of their environment. In other words, we can only reproduce things we have been exposed to either at home, in our circle, inner-circle, and mini-circle.

When it comes to unlearning criminal activities, one has to be proactive, decisive, and most of all have a supporting community that is willing to invest, forgive, and create opportunities for second chances. What I am saying is an unsupported released offender is fragile and vulnerable to his or her former lifestyle without an excellent rehabilitation program.

Anyway, I am inclined to compare the criminal enterprise with the different degrees people earn within an academic setting. For instance, in the justice system, there are probation, misdemeanor, and felony with different degrees, which include death penalty.

On the other hand, there are certificate, diploma, associate, bachelor, master, and doctorate degrees. Being on death row is like having a doctorate in the "criminal institution." It is the highest punishment a human being can receive like a doctorate in the scholastic world.

I do not think some people were born with criminal gene like others seem to imply. Humans have the potential to be good or bad depending on his or her environment. Criminal behaviors are learned as well as good ones.

Based on my tenure and my overall observation and research of the United States Justice System, it seems that once an individual completed serving his or her time in any prison, that person is most likely to go back into the system in less than a year or maximum three years. "Forty-four percent of released prisoners were arrested during the first year following release."[28]

I think in order for the pendulum to shift, law makers should amend certain legislations and start seeing incarcerated individuals as people and not as numbers. They should also begin looking at the bigger picture, which is the society. It is bizarre for the most prosperous country to have the largest incarceration in the world.

It appears that something is not working as it should with the rehabilitation program within the American justice system. A reform is definitely needed and not a band-aid solution in order to understand fully what is not working. Without an intentional and effective prison reform, the vicious incarceration cycle is here to stay.

---

[28] https://bit.ly/3qkAS9n - Access date: 2.12.2021

Conclusion about Juvenile and Death Row Security Facilities

Most inmates are extremely observant. It could be because they have nothing but time on their hands. They watch staff's movements and how some of them interact with some inmates, look for anything out of the ordinary, and try to use it for their own benefit as they have nothing to lose.

I had the honor of working in all the units of that prison. Each of them was different because their residents' spiritual needs varied. The death row unit, however, was my favorite one because there seemed to have been a sense of genuineness during pastoral conversations where they appeared to be willing to discuss certain emotional issues. On the other hand, I felt like other inmates seemed to try to impress staff with stories, as most of them had a release date.

Going to prison has the potential to change someone's life positively or to make that person a *better* skillful criminal. For some youngsters, serving time is like attending classes in a school system where many learn some new skills with the hope to be more well-organized in their criminal activities.

During my tenure at one of the juvenile's facilities, for instance, some juveniles seemed to think that they were criminals in training. They never saw a way out from their environment upon release. Many of them admitted that being exposed to drugs, gangsterism, and criminal activities are the only life they knew. Unfortunately, that same mindset was parallel within the adult prison system.

Biological fathers seemed to be absent in almost all the juveniles I had the privilege to pastor. Some of them never met their biological fathers. For many, their fathers were also serving time. Still, there were those who knew their fathers with no father-and-child relationship. In all those cases, unfortunately, mothers had to play two roles. Hence, there were countless instances where grandparents had to step in to be parents for their grandchildren where one parent or parents were incarcerated simultaneously.

Without those mothers or fathers, grandpas and grandmas, things could have been worse for those parentless children whose while their parents are serving time. Based on my professional experiences, many of the juveniles and adults' inmates I had the privilege of working with were raised by their grandparents. As a result, I am inclined to conclude that in many cases humans seem to be able to do an excellent job parenting one generation and not so well with another one.

America has been number one in the world when it comes to citizens incarceration per capita. According to Statista Research Department, "As of May 2021, the United States had the highest prisoner rate, with 639 prisoners per 100,000 of the national population."[29] It seems obvious that something is not working with our justice system. This phenomenon has moved from a national crisis to a chronic one state because the US has been rewarding that trophy almost yearly for the past decades. Unless a conscious effort is made, beginning in households, many children will keep growing without their parents, mostly fathers.

Credits must be given to those mothers and fathers who are playing two roles while the other parent is incarcerated. They are doing their best to meet their children's needs, especially the emotional ones. However, parenting is a two-person mission; therefore, it seems to take two individuals working harmoniously to achieve some goals. For some special children, moreover, it might take a team of proactive community leaders with great intention to make a positive impact.

No matter how gifted a woman may think she is, it will seem almost impossible to teach a boy how to be a gentleman, and the

---

[29] https://bit.ly/3s22v7S - Access date: 12.17.2021

opposite is true for a man to teach his daughter how to be a lady. That is the reason two is better than one when it comes raising a human being.

At the end of the day, the choice is theirs because in order for changes to take place there must self-examination, admission of wrongdoings, and actions to be taken to amend behaviors. For instance, I always believe that taking an alcoholic to an Alcoholics Anonymous meeting is a waste of time because that person must acknowledge first and foremost there is a problem. In other words, effective change begins within and not with outside forces. Without those elements, a cycle will keep repeating itself.

Dying Naturally on Death Row

During my tenure at that maximum-security prison, there were about five death row inmates who died of natural causes. The chaplain team always organized memorial services to honor their lives on that unit. Afterall, most of them call each other brothers or uncles to the older ones. There was a level of respect for senior inmates from younger ones.

They saw themselves as families. For instance, some of them would ask me if I could check on one of their fellow inmates in that prison's hospital after medical procedure while recovering. There seemed to have a level of caring in their midst.

One day, after informing a death row inmate of the death of one of his family members in the free world, he told me that he did not care because all of his loved ones were here with him. He declined a phone call even though per that prison's SOP he was allowed one.

After assisting him to unpack that statement, he told me that all of his families abandoned him after his death sentence. He made several attempts to keep a line of communication via the postal service system, but never received a reply. After all, he was able to voice his overdue frustrations in a non-judgmental environment during some pastoral sessions.

Whenever there was a natural in-house death, we made ourselves available to provide pastoral counseling especially to those who were close to the deceased. Many of them told me that how they wished to die of natural cause rather than by lethal injection.

After working with juveniles and adults in the minimum-and-maximum security facilities, I learned many lessons in order to be an effective correctional pastoral care provider or employee. A few of the most pertinent were:

1) Being fair, firm, and consistent would go a long way while working with inmates!
2) Showing any type of favoritism in a penitentiary is a recipe for disaster. For instance, if you cannot be nice to all, do not attempt to be with one.
3) When it comes to consistency, make sure to treat them all the same!
4) If you were going to do a favor for an inmate, be prepared and ready to do it for all because it would be a matter of time before the inmate population knew about it via "inmate.com" as they call it.
5) Treat them with respect and dignity should be in the forefront of everything one does around offenders!
6) Losing freedom does not translate to losing respect and dignity!
7) When it comes to behaviors, juveniles and adult inmates are the same. The only difference is that those serving time in adult facilities have experiences and bigger muscles.
8) Do not promise anything if you will not be able to keep it!
9) Offenders master the art of complimenting especially ladies no matter their physical appearances.
10) No matter how terrible things are in your home, keep private life private!
11) Caring offenders could be the most dangerous ones!

12) Most of the inmates I had the privilege to work with were very smart; unfortunately, they used their smartness in criminal activities.
13) In many cases, offenders tend to have ulterior motives when they ask questions or offer compliments.
14) Complacent correctional staff are the most vulnerable and can put a penitentiary in jeopardy. Never be too relaxed!
15) Losing security control of a prison could lead to deadly chaos in a heartbeat.
16) Paradoxically, prisoners seem to lose their freedom in the free world but appear to gain power behind walls.
17) Some adults' offenders are like juveniles with bigger muscles when it comes to their level of thinking.
18) Inmates tend to prey on correctional staff who may seem to be struggling with low self-esteem or self-image.
19) The American society appears to have a parenting problem that reflects in incarceration.
20) Never accept anything as a gift from offenders!

Chapter Eighteen

The Battle for Superiority

Since the beginning of time, the human race has been able to overcome one struggle after another. Human beings are gifted with some level of resiliency to beat the odds when they emerge. There seems to be one scuffle, however, that many people have had difficulty mastering, which is the battle for superiority.

It seems natural that a majority of people want to feel loved, important, and special, which may lead to a stronger self-esteem or self-worth. There is a danger, though, when some try to boost their self-esteem and self-perception by putting down or demonizing other individuals.

In my four decades and plus of living on this planet, I have had the privilege to reside in several countries and be exposed to diverse cultures since my early twenties. One of my passions is interacting and fellowshipping with people. It helps me in the process of understanding others and oneself while building and enhancing healthy relationship with my fellow sojourners.

My purpose is not to point finger on any particular ethnic or social group, but to raise a fundamental issue with regards to human relationship. In fact, as far as I am concerned, humanity has only one race, as the popular cliché puts it, *the human race.*

During my academic pursuit, I have had the opportunity to interact with many citizens from different countries in the Caribbean, and different ethnic groups in the United States of America. My experience has been an interesting one, to say the least.

For instance, while living in the Caribbean I have never thought I would have witnessed prejudice, colorism, and bigotry due to the fact that most people living there are of African descent. I have experienced it first-hand due to my brown complexion or where I was born.

Many brown people with lighter complexion tend to feel more important or beautiful. Alas, some companies, for example, tend to favor potential employees with lighter skin or smoother hair over their counterpart, even though the darker complexion candidates with natural hair could be more qualified.

Even within the Caribbean, some countries tend to think that they are better than the others. They would use anything possible to enhance their image while putting their neighboring countries down. This type of attitude, preference, and myth can be traced all the way back to the colonization period. Unfortunately, it has been thought that people with less pigmentation are smarter and more civilized.

When I arrived in the United States of America for graduate school, I was expecting to find or witness a completely different ball game, simply because it is where the "States are United," so I thought.

Hence, the third US President, Thomas Jefferson, who was also one of the founding fathers, penned in the declaration of independence in 1776 stated that all people are created equal. Those words might be ideal but do not necessarily reflect the actual fact.

To be clear, since I have been living in the United States of America, as a Caribbean person, I have not experienced any racism or prejudice directly, so far. That does not mean I am ignoring its existence, or I am being naïve. It could simply mean that I have not lived here long enough, or I do not know what to look for. It could also mean that I just ignore any racist or discriminatory statements or actions when they reveal themselves.

I must admit, however, since living here, I have been witnessing the "Divided States of America" instead of a "United States." I have noticed that battle throughout the American coasts. Northerners, for instance, claim that they are better, more civil, and more inclusive than southerners. Citizens from the east coast tend to exhibit a sense of pride over those living in the western part of the country and vice versa.

Sadly, even within African descents, some tend to see themselves better than those who live in the continent of Africa or anywhere else in the world simply because they are citizens of the United States of America.

The usage of the term "white" or "black" to some people is pejorative because no human being reflects either color. As a matter of fact, a tire is black, and the snow is white. People from African descent are brown and those from Europe are Caucasian. There is no such thing as black and white skin color. It is a deceit to create division. Unfortunately, many have fallen into that non-sense.

In the political realm, political parties use whatever means necessary to demonize each other. Those on the right think they are better than those on the left and vice versa. Many politicians would use anything in their power to tear down their challengers, even fake information. Unfortunately, extremists are used to fan the flame of divide.

There are those who use their ethical, familial, social, financial, political, educational, ecclesiastical, and religious connotation or affiliation to show others how much better off they are. It seems like "us" versus "them" mentality, which is detrimental for the human race.

The battle for superiority is also active even behind prison walls. Case in point, juveniles who were sentenced less time saw themselves better than those with longer sentences. Hence, they even tried to find superiority in the gravity of their crimes. On the other hand, adult inmates with release dates think they are better than lifers and those waiting to be executed. Strangely, those serving life see themselves superior to those on death row because they will die of natural cause and not by lethal injection.

During my tenure as the death row chaplain, a new inmate shared how uncomfortable he was being among so many murderers and felt that he did not belong there. As a result, he did everything he could to not associate with them.

However, he said that one day he had a light bulb moment realizing that he himself was on the death row unit as a murderer and he was no better than those inmates who killed more people than he did. He concluded that murder is murder no matter what.

This division is spreading everywhere like a deadly cancer throughout our world. It will chip away our humanity slowly but surely if we are not careful and intentional in our interaction with people.

Segregation ended *on paper* with the Civil Rights Acts of 1964 under the 36th president of the United States of America, Lyndon B. Johnson. Before then, brown people were treated like second class citizens in their country of birth. Yes, the apparent segregation has ended but nowadays the pendulum has shifted a little bit. For instance, one's zip code or the amount of taxes paid can sometimes, determine the kind of social services some people may receive, such as a simple road paving, a good school system, water usage, and beautification of parks and recreations where innocent children can play.

This 'social disease' is spreading fast in our culture and the world at large; and it seems very contagious. The last place one would expect to witness or experience bigotry is in a church. Yes, it is in churches.

Whether it is intentional or otherwise, some church goers might give a person a weird look if sitting in a particular pew or chair because many people know that this section is for a specific family. As a result, I have come to realize that the Church is an extension of our society. There is no doubt that as the society goes so does the Church. The late Dr. Martin Luther King Jr. was right when he said, "Sunday morning at eleven o'clock is the most segregated hour in America."[30]

I would go further to add that the ecclesiastical segregation seems to be a universal challenge and it looks like it goes beyond Sunday morning worship services. Many Caucasian churches, for instance, would not call or hire a qualified brown clergy as their local pastor even within the same denomination and vice versa. Within the church context, some Caucasian churches tend to project themselves as better organized and structured than their brown counterparts. The latter one, on the other hand, oftentimes wonders if Caucasian churches are spiritual simple because their worship style is different.

Some churches use speaking in tongues as a way to show how connected they are to God. Still, there are those that boast about their building, membership, and size of their bank account while neglecting the social needs of their parishioners and communities. The battle for superiority exists even in the least expected place, a religious setting.

Using skin color, political views, and place of origin as ways to show superiority goes against humankind. Humans are more important than those things mentioned above. People should be assessed by what they can offer in order to make our world better and not by mundane and useless appearances.

The battle for superiority has its origin in pride. The late prophet Muhammad (*peace be upon him*) stated, "Pride is to distain the truth out of self-conceit and contempt people."[31]

The feeling of superiority appears to be a sign of ignorance, arrogance, and pride. According to Proverbs chapter 21 verse 4

---

[30] https://nyti.ms/32n2YZJ - Access date: 9.20.2021
[31] https://bit.ly/3EhAvkU - Access date: 10.2.2021

from the Christian holy Bible, "Haughty eyes and a proud heart, the lamp of the wicked, are sin."[32]

After witnessing and sometimes experiencing, directly or indirectly, this social fight in different countries and cultural contexts, I am inclined to conclude that people with low-esteem, ignorance, lack of social education, and exposure have the tendency to put others down in order to feel good about themselves just because they have nothing else to valorize themselves.

"According to a 1998 study published in the Scientific American, there are about five thousand ethnic groups worldwide."[33] The human race is made of people with different shades of skin reflectance depending on the distance between our location and the equator. This type of unique diversity can really make our world a better place in terms of strength, as we are part of the same race. The bottom line is, we are all people of colors.

"Ignorance breeds fear. We fear those things we do not understand. If we do not keep that fear in check, that fear in turn, will breed hatred. Because we hate those things that frighten us. If we do not keep that hatred in check, that hatred in turn, will breed destruction. We want to destroy those things, that we hate. Why? Because it causes us to be afraid."[34] *Daryl Davis, an American R&B and blues musician, activist, author, actor, bandleader, met, and talked to Ku Klux Klan (KKK) leader about race.*

Many people have been praying and hoping that one day we all will be able to live in peace and harmony with one another. I hope I do not sound too pessimistic, but I do believe this mêlée will end when the human race ceases.

---

[32] NIV
[33] https://bit.ly/3J7QcyR - Access date: 10.2.2021
[34] https://bit.ly/3sqrUtX - Access date: 10.2.2021

As the golden rule reminds us that we should treat other people the way we want to be treated. Until we start seeing people as we see ourselves, spending time, and fellowshipping with them, the battle for superiority will remain. After all, most of us, if not all, are heading toward the same destination, that is, six feet under or turn into ashes. At the end, the battle for superiority has nothing to do with *skin* color, politics, and place of birth, but pride, which has its origin in *sin*.

Chapter Nineteen
Through It All

My conception and birth were not welcomed by some in my family of origin. During my formative years, however, my presence was finally accepted as I was here to stay. Nevertheless, I was determined not to start my academic voyage in a rural community. As a result, in the summer of 1980, my family migrated to Cap-Haitien, Haiti, where everything started with my learning quest.

On January 17, 2000, I arrived at NCU, Mandeville, Jamaica, with the hope to study Business Administration and minor in Information Technology. However, on Friday, June 25, 2004, I graduated from one of the best theological seminaries, JTS, Kingston, Jamaica, after interpreting a dream about ministry.

On Friday, May 14, 2010, I had the privilege of graduating from one of the most distinguished divinity schools in the USA, CUDS, Buies Creek, NC. Moreover, with the assistance of some great organizers' friends, my wife, Nelcie and I made our love public the next day and had a combo celebration.

At the end of my master's degree in divinity, I realized that I still had a long way to go when it came to theological study and understanding. About two years later, I started the process of enrolling in a doctoral program with that same school. Everything was going well until I met with one of my mentors to request a recommendation letter. He discouraged me from pursuing my dream and said that he thought I would be satisfied with a master's degree. I told him that I believed in continuing education. About a week later, a mutual friend of ours wanted to meet for lunch. It did not take me long to figure it out that the mentor had sent him on a mission to convince me not to proceed with the doctoral program.

Anyway, I proceeded with my application with the intention to ask someone else for that recommendation letter. Weeks later, however, my wife and I became pregnant with our second son, Edwards. After some thinking, praying, and pondering, I concluded that, at the moment, it was not suitable to be engaged in a such demanding academic degree. Therefore, I chose the wellbeing of my young family over post-graduate study. Working full-time, volunteering at a local church as an associate pastor, having a 2-year-old boy, a pregnant wife, and engaging in doctoral research would be a recipe for bitterness and disaster, which could eventually lead to chaos.

About four years later, I revived my academic ambition, and enrolled in the Doctor of Philosophy in Christian Counseling program with Newburgh Theological Seminary, Newburgh, IN. However, halfway through the doctoral research, my sister-in-law suddenly died, and months prior during a casual conversation she asked my wife and I to raise her sole son if she were to die. Days later, she made her request known via a text message.

As a result, I was granted a year off to focus on providing emotional support to my spouse and for my family to adjust with an unexpected member in our family. Since I knew my wife, it was the first time I witnessed her became so emotionally distraught. She lost both a sister and her best friend. Through that experience, I have learned that I could not be a husband and a pastoral care provider simultaneously.

Ten years later, on May 15, 2020, my wife and I celebrated ten years of marriage with our three sons, and less than one month later on June 6, 2020, I received a doctorate in philosophy with a specialization in Christian counseling from a great school, NTS, Newburgh, Indiana. Unfortunately, due to the worldwide outbreak of the COVID-19 pandemic, no graduation was held for the 2020 graduating class. My sons were disappointed because they were looking forward to traveling to another state.

It is finished!

The doctoral program was a long, rigorous, and yet productive process with countless sleepless nights and myriad of hours in libraries and most importantly it would have been impossible without my wife's support and my sons' understanding.

When some people ask if I am the first person in my family of origin to earn a doctorate in philosophy, PhD. I always tell them my parents were the first; and when they inquire in what field of study, I usually answer "in the area of common sense and wisdom." They are my heroes. My dad used to say that one of the fascinating things about knowledge is the fact that it is in your brain, nobody can see, and with it you make money. People can steal your wealth, but they cannot steal your knowledge. Therefore, invest in your brain.

My parents grew up with limited education. Therefore, farming was one of their few options. Looking back, I observed that though they owned lands, they exposed us to education instead of following their footsteps in farming like other children in our rural community. They wanted a different lifestyle for us.

When I reflect on my parents' life, their values, and lessons they instilled in us as their children, I have come to realize that formal education was their main priority. They were determined for us to surpass them in life. They, in return, considered this to be their success.

Through it all, I encountered some difficult moments. I jumped over many hurdles. Countless doors were closed on my face. There were many ups and downs in my personal, professional, ministerial life, and academic career but through it all, God was faithful even though there were countless moments of discouragement.

While examining my academic voyage, I have realized that unless an ambitious student is part of the "one percenter" in this world, student's life always will be challenging. In other words, the "one percent student" does not go through campus hardship. Interestingly, those challenges can make or break some students' ambition if they lose focus of their bigger picture. Having said that, most college students should receive a certificate in management at the end of their studies because it takes a lot of managing to make ends meet or survive campus life in general.

Through it all, I asked God to keep me grounded in His wisdom and helped me to stay connected with His people while climbing the educational ladder. I prayed that same prayer throughout because a little education if not careful could make someone prideful and view those with limited or no formal learning as less valuable citizens.

The late 26th President of the United States, Theodore Roosevelt was allegedly said, "People do not care how much you know until they know how much you care."[35] From my experience, knowledge is important but building human relationship is utmost essential. Having knowledge with no humanity is useless and can at times be dangerous.

This has been a challenging and rewarding academic voyage, which lasted twenty years for now. I have learned many valuable lessons. There were good and not so good days. There were thoughts of giving up. One crucial lesson, however, that I will always keep in mind over those two decades of studies is I am still ignorant in many areas.

Through it all, I have come to realize that education does not make people rich, but it gives them options and alternatives and with those come possibilities. It sometimes can help people to work smarter and not harder.

---

[35] https://bit.ly/3H9XVuw - Access date: 11.11.2021

What More Can I Say?...Let us Pray!

May we always find wisdom, peace, patience, and comfort on our voyage as we examine life's seasons to find God's footprints through His people.

God Bless…Edisson Etienne